The Seven Big Questions

The 7 Big Questions
Searching for God, Truth, and Purpose

Cover art by RipplEffect
Interior layout by Jessica Burnham
Edited by Auburn Layman

Printed in the United States
10 9 8 7 6 5 4 3 2 1
ISBN 978-1-68316-020-5

The 7 Big Questions series is a product of Explore God, a
Global Media Outreach ministry. For more information,
please visit www.ExploreGod.com

The Seven Big Questions
Searching for God, Truth, and Purpose

Bruce B. Miller
Global Media Outreach

This book is dedicated to all who are searching
—and the One to whom we turn when we
don't have answers.

Table of Contents

The Importance of Asking Questions

"I don't believe in God," he told me confidently.

"Oh?" I responded. "Why is that?"

"There's no evidence that God exists. No proof that God is anything more than something people made up to make themselves feel better," he said. "And I'm sick of my parents pushing church on me. Even if there was a God, he doesn't deserve my worship. Have you looked around lately? How could there be a good God in control of the world when terrible things happen every day?"

"That's fair," I said. "You're right—the world is full of pain and suffering. It doesn't make any sense."

He paused, briefly surprised to hear something like that coming from a pastor. Then he turned toward me more directly and looked me straight in the eyes. "Then why do you believe in God?" he asked.

It wasn't the first time I'd been asked that question, and it won't be the last. It's always interesting to see people's reactions when they first learn that I'm a pastor. Body language shifts—people sit up straighter or square off their shoulders defensively—and speech patterns change—people begin to watch their language, some becoming overly polite and others borderline hostile. But that day, I could sense that this young man's question was sincere; he really wanted to know my answer. The conversation wasn't a debate, a game, or an argument. There was a tinge of hopeful longing in the tone of his voice, as if to communicate his desire to see something that might point to God's reality. While you're going to have to read the book in your hands to get my answer (hey, you didn't think I'd let you off that easy, did you?), he listened quietly to my response and then asked a follow-up question: *How long will it take me to figure out if God is real or not?*

Honestly, I don't know the answer to that question for him—or for you. Maybe you're pretty skeptical that there's a God out there, but you're curious. Maybe you know you believe in God, but you're not sure how to respond when someone asks you why you do. Here's what I do know: exploring God is a worthy endeavor. Questions like these are worth asking; their answers, worth seeking.

Explore God

Several years ago, I took a trip to see my daughter, son-in-law, and grandchildren down in Austin, Texas. While I was there, I noticed signs all over the place with simple, consistent messaging: "We all have questions. We all wonder. Explore God." There were yard signs in front of people's houses, banners outside of churches, and billboards on the highway. I wondered what in the world was going on. Since Google knows everything, I did a quick search and found ExploreGod.com.

Usually, I'm on a website for only a few seconds, maybe a couple of minutes. But that day I found myself watching video after video, reading article after article. Though the "About Us" section said that Explore God is a team of Christians, I was seeing something I'd never seen on a Christian website before. In the videos, I watched people of different ethnicities, backgrounds, and ages—artists, entrepreneurs, pastors, theologians, writers—tell real stories of their faith journeys. They were all (even the church leaders!) honest about their doubts, transparent about their past and current struggles, and sincere in sharing their responses to the hard questions being asked.

In the articles, I saw a unique approach to sharing Christian answers to tough spiritual questions. Everything was presented casually and conversationally. It felt like I was wrestling through each question with the author instead of just being told what I was supposed to believe was "the" answer. I got the sense that all they wanted to do was enable a person to discover answers through their own exploration of God, the Bible, and faith.

When I found my way to the Explore God Facebook page, I encountered what felt to me to be exactly what they said they were trying to create: a safe, nonjudgmental place to ask hard questions and explore truth. It didn't seem to matter what your background was, where you were in your faith journey, or what you believed (or didn't believe). You were welcome to ask your questions, seek out truth, and explore answers with the community. I could identify with so much of what I saw there. I've asked my share of hard questions about God and the Bible, both before and after becoming a pastor.

Later, I talked with my daughter and learned that her church—along with hundreds of others from over a dozen different denominations—were coming together in a community-wide initiative. They were inviting the whole city to explore some of life's big questions together through a sermon and discussion group series called The 7 Big Questions. Churches were encouraging people of any or no faith to explore God by freely asking questions that they might not usually feel comfortable asking in a traditional religious setting. We all naturally avoid things we fear will cause us to feel shame or embarrassment. Christians may be hesitant to ask because they feel they should already "know" the answers, and they worry that their questions will show a lack of faith. Non-Christians may have had bad experiences with religion in the past and simply don't feel safe giving voice to their curiosities or questions. But the idea here was to shed light on our doubts, not ignore them. I was intrigued.

Two years later, hundreds of churches in the Dallas area—including my own—united to do an initiative like the one I saw in Austin. That fall, we did The 7 Big Questions series in our church through both sermons and discussion groups. Small groups met in homes, coffee shops, and restaurants to watch videos from Explore God and talk about some of the hard spiritual questions. At my house, a group made up of atheists, spiritually minded people, and a Christian couple met every week. The videos sparked rich, challenging conversations. We questioned each other's assumptions—and our own. On those evenings, we laughed and teased each other, but we also shared our hearts. We found ourselves compelled to go deeper and explore more about what we believed and why.

The 7 Big Questions

Though we all have individual struggles, some questions are more universal than others. In this book, we're going to look at seven of the big life questions many of us share, based on Explore God's aptly named series, The 7 Big Questions:

- Does life have a purpose?
- Is there a God?
- Why does God allow pain and suffering?
- Is Christianity too narrow?
- Is Jesus God?
- Is the Bible reliable?
- Can I know God personally?

But let me lower your expectations right from the start. It's unlikely you'll have all your questions answered in this book. In fact, it's much more probable that you'll walk away with follow-up questions, just like the young man I mentioned above. Your doubts may not be eradicated (and you won't be able to completely erase anyone else's either) but hopefully you'll find insights and information that help you discover, rethink, and solidify your beliefs. I'm not here to tell you what to believe or to force you to accept something blindly. It's vitally important that we each take ownership of our faith. It's not enough to believe in something simply because someone told you; there's no depth to that. We must be critical and intentional in pursuing truth and letting the answers we discover inform our beliefs. As Explore God says, it's the realizations we uncover on our own terms that have the potential to transform our lives.

It's the realizations we uncover on our own terms that have the potential to transform our lives.

Jesus himself encouraged his followers to go deeper in their thinking and faith by asking them questions. In fact, the Bible records Jesus asking over 225 different questions.[1] He also said, "Ask and it will be given to you; seek and you will find; knock and the door will be opened to you. For everyone who asks receives; the one who seeks finds; and to the one who knocks, the door will be opened."[2]

I love a particular quote from Russian novelist Fyodor Dostoevsky. He wrote, "I believe in Christ and confess him not like some schoolboy; but my hosanna has passed through a great furnace of doubt."[3] It's from the refining fire of doubt that strong convictions can emerge, forged by the act of pursuing answers to our hard questions.

We all struggle to understand the world around us and the implications of the idea that there is a higher power who created it all. Doubt often gets a bad reputation, especially within Christian settings, but doubt can actually be hugely productive. It can paralyze us, yes, but it can also propel us to seek out truth. Real progress comes from asking questions and earnestly seeking out answers. In my life, the times of deep doubt and earnest questioning have helped me to grow the most—personally, relationally, and spiritually. The process of questioning and exploring answers has the power to open minds, give rise to new ideas, reveal new horizons, and change our lives.

Facing Our Doubts

When we started this book, no one had heard of COVID-19. Few people had ever experienced a quarantine. Almost no one alive had walked through a pandemic. When the World Health Organization declared the novel coronavirus outbreak a global pandemic March 11, 2020, it rocked the world. Everything we knew—everything we accepted as the normal everyday of life—changed. Instead of going to school, work, or church, we sheltered in place. We didn't know if we could safely open the mail, pick up food from restaurants, or go to the doctor. Around the world, we saw major shortages in basic hygiene and medical supplies. The simple act of hugging a family member—or even being in the same room with them—went from a show of affection to a potential threat to their health.

Suddenly, the very air we breathed seemed unsafe. Panic spread, as it often does in the face of fear and uncertainty—especially when coupled with such a loud reminder of our mortality. Our mental health deteriorated. According to the World Health Organization, the global prevalence of anxiety and depression jumped by a "massive 25%."[4] It also had an unavoidable impact on people's thoughts about God and their relationship with faith. According to the *Journal of Economic Behavior & Organization*, "During the early months of the pandemic, Google searches for prayer relative to all Google searches rose by 30%, reaching the highest level ever recorded."[5] Their estimates indicate that by as early as April 1, 2020, more than half of the world population had prayed for an end to the pandemic and coronavirus.[6]

Theologian Paul Tillich wrote, "Doubt is not the opposite of faith; it is an element of faith."

Even before the pandemic, nearly every Christian, (including me) experienced seasons of wrestling with serious doubts and questions about their faith. That process often takes one deeper in their exploration of

God. Theologian Paul Tillich wrote, "Doubt is not the opposite of faith; it is an element of faith."[7] While you're here with us, we invite you to embrace your doubts, ask your questions, and seek out truth. Not every question you ask will have a clear answer. Mystery abounds in this life, and there are spiritual realities that exceed our understanding. But I agree with theologian Peter Abelard when he said, "Constant and frequent questioning is the first key to wisdom. . . . For through doubting we are led to inquire, and by inquiry we perceive the truth."[8]

Neither I nor Explore God is here to tell you the answers to your questions. We're here to help guide you on your journey to discover truth as you explore God for yourself. So let's get started.

Endnotes for Introduction

1. Roy Zuck, *Teaching as Jesus Taught* (Eugene, OR: Wipf and Stock Publishers, 2002), 237.

2. *The Holy Bible*, New International Version © 2011, Matthew 7:7–8.

3. Fyodor Dostoevsky in his last notebook (1880–1881) as quoted in K. A. Lantz, *The Dostoevsky Encyclopedia* (Greenwood Publishing Group, 2004), 357.

4. "COVID-19 pandemic triggers 25% increase in prevalence of anxiesty and depression worldwide," World Health Organization, March 2, 2022, https://www.who.int/news/item/02-03-2022-covid-19-pandemic-triggers-25-increase-in-prevalence-of-anxiety-and-depression-worldwide.

5. Jeanet Sinding Bentzen, "In crisis, we pray: Religiosity and the COVID-19 pandemic," *Journal of Economic Behavior & Organization*, vol. 192 (2021), 541–583, doi:10.1016/j.jebo.2021.10.014. This report is based on daily and weekly data on Google searches for 107 countries.

6. Ibid. Prayer searches remained 10% higher than previously throughout 2020, particularly so in Europe and the Americas.

7. Paul Tillich, *Systematic Theology*, vol. 2 (Chicago: University of Chicago Press, 1975), 116–117.

8. Peter Abelard, as translated in *Frank Pierrepont Graves, A History of Education During the Middle Ages and the Transition to Modern Times* (1918), 2005 edition, 53.

CHAPTER ONE

Does Life Have a Purpose?

"The dreams in which I'm dying are the best I've ever had."
—*"Mad World," Tears for Fears*[1]

How many of us have identified with this sentiment at some point in our lives? The above lyric hits a common vein of fear that runs through all of us. We may hope—or even usually believe—that there is a reason for us to be here, but sometimes when we lie awake at night, we worry that life has no real meaning. We fear there's no purpose in all our straining and striving. In these times, if you're anything like me, you might ask yourself, *What's the point?*

Fyodor Dostoevsky once wrote, "The secret of man's being is not only to live but to have something to live for."[2] Merely surviving doesn't satisfy our need to live with a sense of purpose. Everyone wants their life to have meaning. But wanting something doesn't make it real. So the question remains: Does life have a purpose?

I encounter this question even in the best of times. A good example is the weekend my wife, Tamara, and I flew to Boston to visit our son Jimmy. Emily, his wife, had just given birth to our first grandson, Theodore James Miller—Theo for short. There was something profound about seeing my son holding his son. The joy was profound and pervasive—beyond words. But so was the overwhelming reminder of the brevity of life.

Frankly, it feels weird to be a grandfather. I'm too young for that . . . right? (Just tell me yes.) I know we all get older, but it still surprises me to notice that I'm aging. These days I look in the mirror and think, *Who is that?* My mental picture of myself doesn't match the person I see in the mirror. Life goes by quickly. One of my good friends recently lost his dad. At the memorial service, people spoke about who he was and what he had done; it was a beautiful celebration of his life. I found myself wondering, *When they put me in the ground, what will they say? Will my life have had any real meaning? Will I have made a difference?* Sometimes late at night those questions urgently whisper to me: Have I lived my life well? Has my life mattered?

Thoughts of Suicide

I remember first seriously questioning life's purpose in the spring of my freshman year of high school. Like many teenagers, I went through a dark time. In those days, I struggled to find anything that made life worth living. It seemed that the world was full of so much pain and suffering—and always would be. At that point, I had few friends and didn't fit in well anywhere. I wasn't an athlete nor was I making great grades. I thought to myself, *You go to high school, hoping to get into college. You graduate, hoping to get a job. You get married, hoping to have kids, just to send them off to school. Then you get old and die. What's the point?*

My Christian background didn't help me embrace life—after all, the Bible teaches that it's better to be with God in heaven than down here on earth. I seriously considered taking my own life. One day I finally explained to my dad what I was thinking. I told him it seemed better to die than to live, and I shared with him my thought that we all might as well get to heaven as soon as possible. My dad affirmed my feelings—both about the pain in the world and the promise of something better than this life. But then he pointed out that if I was basing my thoughts of heaven on the Bible, I also had to consider what it had to say about life here on earth. God tells us to live for others, and ultimately suicide is a tragic choice that no one should make. There's no rushing out of this world without causing others the pain you're trying to escape. His words made sense to me. I'm thankful every day that I did not make that choice.

But despite this personal realization, some years later the question of life's purpose weighed heavily on me once again during my doctoral work at the University of Texas at Dallas. My studies focused on postmodernism, and I drank deeply of deconstruction and critical theory. We read Jacques Derrida and Friedrich Nietzsche, among others. With the tools of critical theory, we deconstructed every worldview and metanarrative that attempted to make sense of this life. For a time, it seemed to me that no philosophy, religion, or worldview entirely held water. They were all suspect, all subject to critique. Each was merely one point of view, influenced by its author's culture and largely contingent on its place in history. Nietzsche, with his bold nihilism that courageously faced the darkness of nothingness, seemed the most honest: We live. We die. That's it.

So which is it? Does life have a purpose, or is there no point to all this? Is the church answer—that of course there is a higher purpose here—true? But if that's the case, why does life so often feel empty?

Facing the Question

These are very real questions that press on many people around the world, and they have throughout history. Sometimes the questions arises in a moment of crisis. Other times, they come from a place of fatigue or utter boredom with everyday life. Even if you're not wondering about life's purpose right now, you likely have at some point. Or maybe a friend has been asking some version of this question, and you want to help her wrestle with it and find answers.

If it's not something you're struggling with at the time, it can be all too easy to dismiss someone else's doubts, questions, and concerns. You want to tell them to quit worrying, to accept that there are some things we will never understand. And when you're the one asking the question, it's tempting to busy yourself with work and family and hobbies, trying to distract yourself enough to avoid the issue. Today it's easier than ever to dodge serious questions by spending our free time engaging with our ever-present screens instead of the life around us. But dismissing someone's fears or hiding from your own struggles doesn't help anyone.

An Unexpected Response from the Bible

You may already be rolling your eyes at the mention of the Bible. You may not believe that it's a source of reliable truth—and that's OK. There's a whole chapter on that coming up, so just go with me here for a bit.

The Bible takes the question of life's purpose seriously. In fact, an entire book is devoted to the subject. It's called Ecclesiastes, and it's quite an intriguing text. The speaker in Ecclesiastes—likely King Solomon—actually answers the question with a resounding *no*. "Meaningless! Meaningless!" the writer says. "Utterly meaningless! Everything is meaningless."[3] Well, I don't know about you, but that's not what I expected from the Bible.

Like many of us, Solomon feels that life doesn't offer any permanent satisfaction. You get a girlfriend. At first you think she'll make you happy, but pretty soon the romance fades. You're making money and feeling pretty good about it, but then you hear about your friend's raise. Suddenly you feel inadequate. You make the team, but you lose the championship. You buy things. You get the promotion. You do all the things you're supposed to do. And so what? None of it keeps you happy forever. Nothing satisfies permanently. You still experience sneaking feelings of emptiness, of incompletion, of discontent. Or maybe it's the monotony of life that gets to you. Another diaper to change, another deal to close, another dinner to make. The daily grind is mind-numbing and overwhelming. It's easy to begin to lose any sense of a greater purpose.

An Echo in Music

Many great works of literature, music, and film reflect the despair we feel when we fail to find meaning in life. A number of contemporary songwriters have questioned life's purpose, wondering if anything in life really matters. Some of them sound a lot like Solomon in Ecclesiastes. Let's take a look at just a few.

"Changes," Tupac

"I see no changes. Wake up in the morning and I ask myself, 'Is life worth living? Should I blast myself?'"[4] Pretty depressing stuff, right? Well, whether he knew it or not, Tupac was echoing a sentiment Solomon expressed thousands of years before: "And I declared that the dead, who had already died, are happier than the living, who are still alive."[5] Doesn't sound very "Christian," but there you have it.

"Bohemian Rhapsody," Queen

Queen anticipated Tupac's questions in their 1975 song: "Is this the real life? Is this just fantasy? Caught in a landslide, no escape from reality. . . . Nothing really matters; anyone can see. Nothing really matters; nothing really matters to me."[6] Sound familiar? Queen's final lines sound a lot like Solomon's refrain of "meaningless."

"Dust in the Wind," Kansas

"Just a drop of water in an endless sea. All we do crumbles to the ground, though we refuse to see. Dust in the wind. All we are is dust in the wind."[7] Back in my years of teen anguish, I sang these words with deep adolescent angst. Kansas's famous song sounds remarkably like several passages from Ecclesiastes, such as, "The wind blows to the south and turns to the north; round and round it goes, ever returning on its course."[8]

Listening with Compassion

At some moment in your life, you may have hit a spot where everything seemed pointless and you sang lyrics like these in the dark. Maybe that time is now; your heart is singing these words, shouting a refrain that bemoans the meaninglessness of life. Perhaps it's not you but a loved one who is struggling to find meaning, who feels they're staring into the void. No matter who in your life is asking this question, it's crucial that you pay attention to these concerns and listen with patience and compassion—even if that means listening to yourself.

Often this particular question comes from a place of deep pain. Tragedy, failure, and loss propel us to dark reflection. All of life's turning points, even the happy ones—marriage, graduation, the birth of a child—can cause this question to bubble to the surface. What's the point of it all—all that hard work? Late at night when you can't sleep and have nothing to distract you, an unsettling feeling of emptiness can descend on you. After a great success, the emotional high eventually evaporates. Valleys follow mountaintops, and these times can lead to anxiety, depression, and even self-harm.

Instead of rushing to slap a Bible verse Band-Aid on the pain or trying to find solace in some greeting card cliché, take the time to listen to the *why* behind your thoughts or your friend's fears. Be compassionate—with yourself and with others. That means taking the time to listen and really *hear*, to be quiet and focus on the murmurings of the heart. It's not a time to argue or answer; it's a time to pay attention and strive to understand.

Trapped in Your Own Life

Life is relentless. No matter how many items you cross off your to-do list, you're never really done. There's always more to do—and often you wind up doing the same things over and over again. Do you know what I mean? Sometimes I feel stuck in a continuous cycle. My alarm clock wakes me up at 5:30 a.m. I take a shower, get dressed, grab a quick breakfast, and rush out the door to get to the office. I log in to the computer, answer e-mails, handle messages, break for lunch, and then head back to work. Throw in some meetings for good measure. At 6:00 p.m., I shut down, get back in the car, drive home, get dinner, and clean up. Since my kids are grown, I no longer have to get the kids to bed, so I have time to watch a little TV with my wife before I fall asleep. All that just to wake up at 5:30 and do it again.

Can you relate? You may feel trapped in your own life, like Phil Connors in the movie *Groundhog Day*. Bill Murray plays Phil Connors, an arrogant TV weatherman who finds himself stuck in a time loop repeating the same day over and over again. No matter what he tries to do differently to break the cycle, he wakes up each morning in the exact same day. Sometimes when we are caught in the routines of life, we imagine that if we only had enough money or opportunity, we could break out and find a meaningful life.

A Surprising Experiment

Solomon had that option. When he lived, he was the wealthiest, most powerful man in the world. In Ecclesiastes 2, he summarizes some of his pursuits. Look at the range of things he tries with virtually unlimited money and power:

> I said to myself, "Come now, I will test you with pleasure to find out what is good." But that also

proved to be meaningless. "Laughter," I said, "is madness. And what does pleasure accomplish?" I tried cheering myself with wine, and embracing folly—my mind still guiding me with wisdom. I wanted to see what was good for people to do under the heavens during the few days of their lives. I undertook great projects: I built houses for myself and planted vineyards. I made gardens and parks and planted all kinds of fruit trees in them. I made reservoirs to water groves of flourishing trees. I bought male and female slaves and had other slaves who were born in my house. I also owned more herds and flocks than anyone in Jerusalem before me. I amassed silver and gold for myself, and the treasure of kings and provinces. I acquired male and female singers, and a harem as well—the delights of a man's heart. I became greater by far than anyone in Jerusalem before me. In all this my wisdom stayed with me. I denied myself nothing my eyes desired; I refused my heart no pleasure. My heart took delight in all my labor, and this was the reward for all my toil. Yet when I surveyed all that my hands had done and what I had toiled to achieve, everything was meaningless, a chasing after the wind; nothing was gained under the sun.[9]

Solomon really goes for it. He lives it up in every way imaginable. He tries success and achievement, completing great projects and building colossal wealth. He "embrace[s] folly"—he drinks; he hires his own singers; he denies himself no pleasure. He even gets himself a harem. (Hey, I told you Ecclesiastes isn't quite what you'd expect to read in the Bible.) But believe it or not, Solomon's stubborn dissatisfaction stays firmly in place. None of it makes a difference in any lasting way. He tries it all, from working hard to playing harder. And what does he find? "Everything was meaningless, a chasing after the wind."[10] Rough stuff.

Life Is Short; Death Is Certain

Solomon's writings get even darker as he begins to reflect on the brevity of life and the inevitability of death. "Surely the fate of human beings is like that of the animals," he writes. "The same fate awaits them both: As one dies, so dies the other. All have the same breath; humans have no advantage over animals. Everything is meaningless. All go to the same place; all come from dust, and to dust all return."[11] Many philosophers echo this sentiment, proposing that all life-forms are equal—meaning human life has no more value than a lion or a lizard or a bacterium. We all return to dust after death.

And can we even say that life is better than death? Solomon doesn't think so, especially since this world is full of suffering: "Better . . . is the one who has never been born, who has not seen the evil that is done under the sun."[12] No warm and fuzzies here, huh? But he doesn't stop there. Solomon points out that after we die, no one remembers us anyway. After a while, no one even remembers our names. Few of us know much about our grandparents' grandparents—and that's just four generations back.

Most of the time, we hide from these realities. We don't want to face the darkness. Many of us know the hollowness, the emptiness beneath the veneer of nice homes or bright smiles or new cars. We can't escape the futility of it all, but we exhaust ourselves trying to keep the illusion alive.

Meaningless, Meaningless

Solomon doesn't dodge the issue of life's difficulty in this cursed and distorted world. In fact, the book opens with a clear complaint about this very thing: "Everything is meaningless. What do people gain from all their labors at which they toil under the sun?" Solomon asks.[13]

Hebel, the Hebrew word translated here as "meaningless," appears thirty-eight times in Ecclesiastes—you may feel like you've seen the word "meaningless" that many times just in this chapter! *Hebel* literally means "vapor," like steam or a cloud. It refers to something that looks solid but dissipates when you try to grab hold of it. It can also be translated as "vanity," as it was in the King James Version of the Bible. (Maybe you've heard the phrase "vanity, vanity"— here's where that saying originates.) *Hebel* eventually came to mean futile, worthless, and even absurd in the sense of incomprehensible. There's no mistaking what Solomon is saying: This world—this life—makes no sense. It's pointless, meaningless, and flat-out incomprehensible.

But (isn't there always a "but"?) Solomon doesn't

stop there. There's one small but hugely significant detail that we can't overlook. Another oft-repeated phrase in his book gives us our biggest clue yet. The phrase "under the sun" is said nearly thirty times in the book, the first occurrence being the verse we just discussed: "What does man gain from all his labor at which he toils *under the sun?*"[14] The phrase refers to life here on earth—where, as we've discussed, nothing quite satisfies.[15] Why is this an important qualification? Well, if we look only at life literally under the sun, down here on this earth, there is no greater purpose. But what if there were something more, something—bear with me here—*above* the sun?

Looking Beyond

Through the book of Ecclesiastes, Solomon helps us see our limitations, our inability to figure out life's purpose, and our own mortality. But with that repeated qualifier of "under the sun," Solomon hints that perhaps there is a lasting sense of purpose to be found elsewhere. Down here, life is absurd, but what if there's more than just what's under the sun?

As a species, we are universally disturbed by the condition of our world. We are horrified by acts of violence and war, distraught when a natural disaster hits, and anxious about our impact on this planet. We're united in our feeling that life isn't supposed to be this way. Something is broken. Something is desperately wrong. In the midst of the chaos, we seek order. And, to a degree, we can find hints of something better in the world—order and design, intricate patterns and reliable rhythms, a logical beauty and a beautiful logic. We can see the goodness of humanity through acts of charity, compassion, and kindness.

But how can this be? Didn't we just establish that nothing here brings us a lasting sense of purpose or belonging? Solomon runs through everything we can think of as a source of success—wisdom, pleasure, work, riches, advancement—and writes them off as meaningless. There must be something more to this life than the dust Solomon laments. If we continue in Ecclesiastes, we begin to glimpse a deeper layer of Solomon's philosophy.

Longing for Eternity

In chapter 3, Solomon writes, "He has made everything beautiful in its time. He has also set eternity in the human heart; yet no one can fathom what God has done from beginning to end."[16] That's a beautiful phrase, isn't it? "Set eternity in the human heart." Solomon means that we all have an innate longing for permanence. We all yearn for something more than this life, something more than just ourselves, something bigger than what we see in the mundane everyday. Remember, this book was written thousands of years ago. But Solomon hits on something that's just as true today as it was before he was born. We all want to outlast death: We build monuments. We write memoirs. We tell our children stories of when we were young. We long to be remembered and escape the darkness of being forgotten.

Humanity has always imagined life after this one, an existence beyond the one being lived. Afterlife narratives are part of our collective culture. We write and consume hundreds of novels and films filled with plots that center on discovering another world or living in an alternate reality—stories envisioning a life beyond or different from this one. We want to reject the idea that this life is all there is. This world isn't right or fair—in Solomon's words, "the righteous . . . get what the wicked deserve, and the wicked . . . get what the righteous deserve."[17]

We think that even though we might not understand all of what happens in life, surely there must be a purpose. There must be a reason. Solomon tries desperately to find a way to make sense of it all:

> I applied my mind to know wisdom and to observe the labor that is done on earth—people getting no sleep day or night. . . . No one can comprehend what goes on under the sun. Despite all their efforts to search it out, no one can discover its meaning. . . . So I reflected on all this and concluded that the righteous and the wise and what they do are in God's hands, but no one knows whether love or hate awaits them. All share a common destiny— the righteous and the wicked, the good and the bad, the clean and the unclean, those who offer sacrifices and those who do not. . . This is the evil in everything that happens under the sun: The same destiny overtakes all.[18]

Could there be a bleaker message? Thankfully, Solomon doesn't quit there. He decides to look beyond what he can see "under the sun." He decides it's worth seeking out a higher purpose for life.

The Bottom Line

In the last chapter of Ecclesiastes (spoiler alert!), Solomon very clearly gives us what he calls "the conclusion of the matter."[19] He writes, "Now all has been heard; here is the conclusion of the matter: Fear God and keep his commandments, for this is the duty of all mankind. For God will bring every deed into judgment, including every hidden thing, whether it is

---

**In God, Solomon tells us,
we can find life's purpose.**

---

good or evil."[20]

We're in for another unexpected twist, because Solomon is saying something profoundly paradoxical. In Solomon's view, it's the promise of divine judgment that gives us hope. This message means that the wicked will no longer get what the righteous deserve, nor the righteous what the wicked deserve. We can derive great meaning and purpose from the news that we will be held accountable for our lives. In short, our lives—what we do, think, and say—matter. The promise of future judgment says that God cares what happens down here under the sun. And from this viewpoint, we're not doomed to a meaningless existence.

We can have hope that wrong will not prevail in the end. There will be justice and reconciliation. The human suspicion that life in this world is not as it was meant to be is founded in truth. In a world where people step on others in their climb to the top and powerful people do what they want seemingly without consequences, divine judgment gives us confidence and reassurance. From Solomon's understanding, God will intervene and set right all that is wrong. Judgment implies justice, intelligence, and a sense of worth—after all, what's the point of fixing something if it doesn't matter? We matter, and our cries for justice will be answered.

That's all well and good, but there's still one glaring question: Why does Solomon tell his readers to "fear God"? We usually consider fear a bad thing, so let's pause for a moment to look at what the concept means in a biblical context. Within the Bible, the "fear of God" combines the ideas of respect and awe, of deep reverence and humble worship. To fear God means to recognize his reality and omnipotence as God.

Proverbs, another book many scholars believe was written mostly by Solomon, says that the fear of the Lord is the beginning of wisdom.[21] What does this mean? It means that, to Solomon, the first step toward wisdom is an acknowledgment that we are not God and that God, well, *is*. It means admitting that we cannot figure out life and live it well on our own—despite our efforts to do just that.

Hints of Purpose

In summarizing the message of Solomon's book, one Bible commentator writes, "Ecclesiastes urges its readers to recognize that they are mortal. They must abandon all illusions of self-importance, face death and life squarely, and accept with fear and trembling, their dependence on God."[22] Solomon unapologetically delivers us from rose-colored delusions about finding purpose in the pursuit of pleasure, success, or wealth and instead points us to the only one who makes life coherent and permanently fulfilling. In God, Solomon tells us, we can find life's purpose. After running down nearly every earthly avenue to find meaning in his life, Solomon looks up to find purpose beyond himself. If God is our ultimate creator, then it makes sense to ask the creator the purpose of his creation. It's sensible to ask the inventor the reason for his invention.

Solomon finds a conviction that God made this world and gave us directions for how to live well in it—what Solomon calls "[God's] commandments." Not only this, but God put eternity in our hearts. If the grave is not the end, then how we live matters not only now but also eternally. Life's ultimate purpose transcends our brief time on Earth. While Solomon never gives a clear statement on what life's purpose is, he points out the path of discovery for us. He warns us of where we will not find purpose and guides us to where we will. He shares that he found his purpose in deep reverence for the God he knew, and he found his hope in the expectation that one day God would set right the world through divine justice.

Knowing and Not Knowing

I surfaced from my struggle with feelings of meaninglessness in those dark days of doctoral work with humble confidence. After examining many other points of view, I came to a place of acceptance regarding the limitations of human knowledge. If there is a higher power, I am not it, and I cannot fathom all that has been and is being done in the world. There is much we cannot know. We don't know exactly how our bodies extract all the nutrients from the food we eat, but we know enough to eat healthy food to help our bodies function. We don't know everything about life or why some things happen, but we can know enough to seek life's purpose beyond us.

Of course, all this assumes there is a God out there. But what if there's not? If there is no God, then he certainly can't have a purpose for life. So which is it? Is there a God, or is there not?

Endnotes for Chapter 1

1. Roland Orzabal, "Mad World," *The Hurting*, Phonogram, released September 20, 1983.
2. Project Gutenberg, *Fyodor Dostoevsky's The Brothers Karamazov*, February 12, 2009, Ebook 28054.
3. *The Holy Bible*, Ecclesiastes 1:2.
4. Tupac Shakur and Deon Evans, "Changes," *Greatest Hits*, originally recorded by Interscope Records in 1992, released October 13, 1998.
5. *The Holy Bible*, Ecclesiastes 4:2.

6. Queen, "Bohemian Rhapsody," *A Night at the Opera*, EMI, released October 31, 1975.

7. Kerry Livgren, "Dust in the Wind," *Point of Know Return*, Kirshner, released January 16, 1978.

8. *The Holy Bible*, Ecclesiastes 1:6.

9. *The Holy Bible*, Ecclesiastes 2:1-11.

10. *The Holy Bible*, Ecclesiastes 2:11.

11. *The Holy Bible*, Ecclesiastes 3:19-20.

12. *The Holy Bible*, Ecclesiastes 4:3.

13. *The Holy Bible*, Ecclesiastes 1:2-3.

14. *The Holy Bible*, Ecclesiastes 1:3, emphasis added.

15. Derek Kidner, *The Message of Ecclesiastes* (Leicester, England: InterVarsity Press, 1976), 23.

16. *The Holy Bible*, Ecclesiastes 3:11.

17. *The Holy Bible*, Ecclesiastes 8:14.

18. *The Holy Bible*, Ecclesiastes 8:16-17, 9:1-3.

19. *The Holy Bible*, Ecclesiastes 12:13.

20. *The Holy Bible*, Ecclesiastes 12:13-14.

21. *The Holy Bible*, Proverbs 9:10.

22. Duane A. Garrett, *The New American Commentary—Proverbs, Ecclesiastes, Song of Songs* (Nashville: Broadman Press, 1993), 278.

CHAPTER TWO

Is There a God?

"What comes into our minds when we think about God is the

Betrayal and heartbreak can make it almost impossible to see any potential for the existence of a just God.

most important thing about us." —A. W. Tozer[1]

"How God thinks of us is not only more important, but infinitely more important. Indeed, how we think of Him is of no importance except in so far as it is related to how He thinks of us." —C. S. Lewis[2]

When our church did The 7 Big Questions series, my wife was gracious enough to open our home to some of my friends for an Explore God Discussion Group—a departure from our usual racquetball games. My friends and I mainly knew each other in gym shorts and protective eyewear, sweating as we chased a little blue ball around the court in (mostly) friendly competition. Between games, the majority of our conversations dipped into topics only as deep as the Dallas Cowboys and the Texas heat. So those nights in our home, listening to my friends and their significant others share their honest thoughts about God, were compelling. People's ideas about God varied wildly. As we shared our thoughts on various spiritual matters over the weeks, we found ourselves clarifying our opinions and even changing our minds through the process of conversation.

Perspectives ranged from the belief that God is something like the energy that connects us to each other to the assertion that though it's a nice idea, there is no God. Others suggested that perhaps God is everything—that our lives are like waves that rise for a time and then settle back into the ocean that is God. One person graciously but firmly shared that he is an atheist, quoting Karl Marx's famous statement that religion is the opiate of the masses. The notion of a God, he said, is a comforting idea that makes people feel better—especially on their deathbed—but it's simply not true.

As we got to know each other better, it became evident that many of our ideas about God came not from intellectual analysis but from life experiences—especially with significant people in our lives. A lesbian friend shared heart-wrenching stories of being attacked verbally and emotionally by Christians. She told us of the pain she felt because of the absence of Christians during the HIV crisis. She personally cared for over a dozen men in a rundown facility, where she witnessed the agony they experienced as their Christian family members rejected them because of their sexual orientation. All they wanted was to hear from mom or dad. But she watched them die without that comfort, and she went to their funerals. That scars the soul.

Other friends shared stories of growing up in damaging religious environments where "faith" was used as an excuse for all kinds of behavior— oppression, neglect, manipulation. Extreme religious experiences can act like walls, blocking any future healthy interaction with religion or spirituality. After such experiences, many understandably want nothing to do with religion and seriously question if there is a God at all.

Difficult life events can stir up doubts in all areas of life, leaving us in deep crises of faith. You got that terrible news and cried out to God to save your baby, but your child didn't survive; you stopped praying because there must not be a God to hear your prayers after all. You lost a parent unexpectedly; now you can't shake that pervasive feeling that you're utterly alone in this life. Or you might relate to my friend and his brother, who were abused by a religious authority figure who was supposed to be a representative of God on earth. Betrayal and heartbreak can make it almost impossible to see any potential for the existence of a just God.

Smoldering doubts over God's existence have been

fanned into flames by recent books written by New Atheists, such as Richard Dawkins's *The God Delusion* and Christopher Hitchens's *God Is Not Good*. Their popularity exposed many to traditional arguments against God's existence, which confirmed some people's suspicions that there is no such thing as God. Most people—Christians included—have had moments when they weren't sure if there was a God. I know I have. Like I mentioned in the last chapter, there was

---

God is more than the conclusion of a logical argument—yet believing in God's existence is not irrational or without evidence.

---

a time when I thought we were creatures who live and die like every other animal, with no ultimate meaning in our lives. Right now, most of us know someone who is asking, "*Is* there a God?"

An Evidence-Based Exploration

On what grounds will we consider the claim for God? Do we just take a blind leap of faith? That would be intellectually irresponsible. But some people—theists and atheists alike—don't want to be confused with new information. They are comfortable with what they think about God right now, and they don't want their beliefs rattled with evidence that might point to a need to rethink their stances. Let's be honest; it's scary to consider we might be wrong about something, especially when it's an issue of such gravity. It takes courage to reconsider what you think and open your mind to possibilities other than what you currently believe.

Over this past summer, my wife and I faced a decision either to buy a new car or to try to make our current one last. "Old Faithful," our grey Ford Taurus Wagon, was giving out. We had hoped it would last another year, but with over two hundred thousand miles on it, we weren't sure it would make it. We wanted to wait until we had enough saved to pay for most of a new car outright, but we weren't even close. How could we know the right choice? If we kept the car and it continued to run, we would save money. If we kept it and it broke down, we'd be in trouble.

We couldn't know for sure what would happen, but we could make an informed decision. We found a retired car repairman who evaluates old cars. He took Old Faithful for a spin and examined her from bumper to bumper, taking dozens of pictures to get a close-up look at every part. He scoured car sites to get expert opinions on our model. In a multi-page report, he detailed every system and summarized his expert advice. The bottom line? We should trade in the car. Its odds of failing soon were high, and when it did, the current limited value would drop to nothing. Then we went to our local Ford dealer, who had serviced Old Faithful for over ten years. They gave the same advice. It was likely (though not certainly) time to get a different car. So we did.

Determining whether or not to buy a new car is by no means an issue of the same weight as deciding if God is real. But I offer this illustration because when it comes to God's existence, many of us demand a higher level of certainty than we have in all other areas of our lives. Though we tend to crave certainty, we are finite human beings and cannot know anything absolutely. In ordinary life, none of us are entirely sure of anything— that we will have a job next year, a place to live in five years, or even wake up tomorrow. We can't be certain that the sun will rise in the morning; it could explode in some rare cosmic event. But we're pretty sure it will be there when we wake up, because so far in our experience, the sun has been in the sky every morning. God is more than the conclusion of a logical argument— yet believing in God's existence is not irrational or without evidence. Sounds paradoxical, I know. You might even think it seems nonsensical. But if you could bear with me for a bit, I'll explain what I mean.

A good analogy comes from the concept of trial by jury, in which jurors are instructed by the judge to determine their verdict beyond a reasonable doubt. In the courtroom, you look for evidence that is sufficiently compelling for you to vote guilty or innocent. This should be kept in mind when exploring God's existence. A person ought to be able to say either, "I am convinced beyond a reasonable doubt that God exists," or "I am convinced beyond a reasonable doubt that God does not exist." Regarding the question at hand, we are looking for sufficiently compelling evidence to decide if there is a God. This doesn't mean all our doubts will be erased forever, but we are examining the evidence rather than taking a blind leap.

As we explore the possibility of God's existence

together, we're going to take a look at four lines of evidence—each like a candle in a darkened room. When it's dark, I have a hard time seeing if someone else is in the room with me; I can't be sure it's not just my imagination. But with each candle I light, the room brightens. I become more confident that there really is another person there, until finally, I can recognize who it is.

An Apostle in Athens

In the first century CE, the Apostle Paul devoted his life to traveling throughout the ancient world to share the gospel. "Gospel" is a word rooted in the Greek *euangelion,* which means "good news." You might see another familiar word in there: evangelize. That's exactly what Paul was doing. He was spreading the word about what he believed to be the truth about God's existence, God's role in our lives, and God's love for humanity.

In Paul's time, Athens, Greece, was the intellectual capital of the world; its rich philosophical tradition stretched all the way back to Socrates, Plato, and Aristotle. The city was a hub for education and thought—imagine Oxford, Cambridge, and Harvard combined. Scholars and philosophers of the day would make speeches and hold debates in the *agora,* the central gathering place for the people. The agora was the nucleus of the artistic, political, and spiritual life of the city. So it makes sense that Paul would have found himself in the middle of the Athens agora, ready to share his news with all those who would listen.

The agora was filled with temples and monuments to the gods of the Greek pantheon. When he arrived in Athens, Paul was "greatly distressed to see the city was full of idols" because he believed there was only one God, not many gods.[3] He even noticed an altar with the inscription: "TO AN UNKNOWN GOD."[4] Nothing if not thorough, the Greeks had erected a monument to

The Big Bang and the biblical concept of creation are not at odds with each other.

any god they may have inadvertently left out, lest they be punished for any omissions. Quite clever, really . . . and it provided Paul the perfect launching point to share his perspective on the issue at hand. "Now what you worship as something unknown I am going to proclaim to you," Paul said, and thus began his speech to the people of Athens as he told them about God.[5]

The Greek word *ágnōstos*, translated here as "unknown," is the root from which we derive the word "agnosticism," the belief that the reality of God is unknown or even unknowable. Perhaps your view of God is a bit agnostic sometimes. You think to yourself, *Maybe there is a God, but I don't know for sure, and I definitely don't know which one it is. How could I?* If so, you're not alone in these thoughts. According to *National Geographic*, there is a global rise in those who claim no religion and identify themselves as either atheist, agnostic, or nonreligious.[6] Many people remain unconvinced either way. As his speech continues, Paul addresses the issue of the unknown by hinting at four lines of evidence for God's existence. We'll develop Paul's thoughts, lighting four candles in the dark room of uncertainty: logic, science, morality, and experience.[7]

Candle #1: Logic

Logic—more specifically, the relationship between logic and existence—is the first candle we'll use to try to light the path to discovery. We're going to begin by taking a look at what is often called the cosmological argument. Cosmology deals with the natural order of the universe, and while this approach can get very philosophical and complex, the fundamental concept alone is compelling.[8] The basic principle of the cosmological argument focuses on causality and the concept of a "first cause." Wondering what that means? Let's dive in.

The Cosmological Argument

Pinch your arm; you can feel that sting. Go for a walk; you can hear your feet on the ground. Bite into an apple; you can taste its sweetness. We know when something exists; our senses confirm the facts. But think beyond that. Why does anything exist in the first place? Why is there something . . . rather than nothing? If there were nothing, it would require no explanation—we wouldn't even be here to try to explain it! But something *does* exist. We exist. Our world exists. The universe exists. And we know that everything that exists has a cause—a point of origin, a beginning. Everything was brought into being somehow. Something cannot be caused by nothing. As *The Sound of Music* puts it, "Nothing comes from nothing. Nothing ever could."[9]

Beyond that, everything in our world is dependent on something else for its existence. Everything needs something else. For example, where I live, the hot summer sun drains the life out of our plants. They desperately need water because they depend on it to live—as does most everything in our world. But where did the water come from? How did the very first droplets fall on the earth? What about the seeds? Who or what created the very first seed? If everything is relying on something else, what is the foundation that supports the whole?

It's common to hear someone ask what is often believed to be an unanswerable question: If God created the universe, then where did God come from? Of course, we could ask the same question of the universe itself. Almost all scientists now agree that, at one time, the universe didn't exist. At a specific moment about 13.7 billion years ago, matter, space, energy, and time came into existence in what is popularly known as the Big Bang. Since the universe has not always existed—that is, it had a beginning—where did the universe come from?

It's important to pause and note here that the Big Bang and the biblical concept of creation are not at odds with each other. On the contrary, whereas many ancient religious books state that matter is eternal and that gods evolved out of that matter, the Bible teaches that God (not matter or the universe) is eternal. For many years, scientists resisted the Big Bang theory—and some still do, in large part because of its implications for intelligent design. If the universe has not always existed, it had to have been created by something. That is, if there was a Big Bang, someone must have pulled the metaphorical trigger. There must be an ultimate cause—what is sometimes known as "the uncaused cause."

The Uncaused Cause

Am I losing you? It's kind of a confusing phrase, I know. All I mean is that if you keep asking the endless "But what created *that*?" question, you end up in a vicious cycle with no exit. Consider this illustration: Draw a circle. The circle represents everything in the universe. Logically, the ultimate cause of everything (meaning the source of the creation of the entire universe) must either be inside or outside of that circle—inside or outside of the universe. Well, we know that everything inside the circle is dependent on something else, so that eliminates an internal cause. We must, then, conclude that the explanation for everything *inside* the circle must be *outside* the circle—a wholly independent cause.

Before Paul entered the scene, both Plato and Aristotle reached similar conclusions. Plato said that there must be an ultimate maker who ordered the primordial chaos into the rational cosmos we observe today. In his book *Metaphysics*, Aristotle argued there must be an unmoved mover—a power that moves things but was not moved by a prior action. For theists, this force of creation—the uncaused cause, ultimate maker, and unmoved mover—is God. Theists believe that God is eternal and has always existed; God is the final answer to the question of creation. As Paul says, God is the maker of heaven and earth, which leads to our next line of evidence: science.

Candle #2: Science

Where do you get a sense that there's something bigger than you out there? I enjoy asking people where they feel close to God or a higher power. It's amazing how many people describe moments in the mountains, surrounded by the grandeur of majestic snow-covered peaks, or beautiful days on the beach, looking out on the endless ocean at sunset. Others feel God in the quiet of a garden, listening to the music of the birds and contemplating the beauty of a blooming rose. As for me, I'll take the mountains. My happy place is high up in the thin, dry air of the Rocky Mountains of Colorado, smelling the pine trees, watching the aspen leaves dancing in the wind, listening to the roar of a stream. The juxtaposition of the tiny, delicate wildflowers and the massive rock cliffs stirs me. I can feel that there is something big going on out there—something more than I can understand.

This second candle might seem surprising since today religion and science are often pitted against each other. However, the idea that science and religion are opposed has not always been the norm; historically the two often worked hand in hand.[10] As Einstein said,

"Science without religion is lame; religion without science is blind."[11] Here we're going to stick to exploring the teleological argument, which is also known as the argument from design.[12] The teleological argument looks at how the world around us reveals the likelihood that our universe was created through deliberate, intelligent design.

The Teleological Argument

Throughout human history, people have looked at the complexities of the world and wondered how it all came to be. Many of even the earliest creation narratives assumed that there was a higher power or master designer—often a God or gods—behind the architecture of our world. But as science advanced and we learned more about our universe, some began to hypothesize that abiogenesis could explain the origin of life. Abiogenesis works to demonstrate how non-living substances ("abio-") created life ("genesis"). Perhaps you've heard of Darwin's "primordial soup." The concept is based on his suggestion that life may have begun in a "warm little pond, with all sorts of ammonia and phosphoric salts, lights, heat, electricity, etc. present, so that a protein compound was chemically formed ready to undergo still more complex changes."[13]

This theory was popular for many years—and still is, among some—but more recently, scientists across multiple disciplines have begun challenging this hypothesis. Many point out that random chance plus time does not equal complex design. In fact, the combination usually creates the opposite: a mess. In

1981, Sir Fred Hoyle and Chandra Wickramasinghe wrote *Evolution from Space,* in which they calculated the odds that the necessary set of enzymes for even the simplest living cell could come together by chance alone.[14] Their final number was one in $10^{40,000}$. As a bit of perspective, the number of atoms in the entire universe is estimated to be 10^{80}. Hoyle compared the likelihood of the random emergence of a single cell to the likelihood that "a tornado sweeping through a junkyard might assemble a Boeing 747 from the materials therein."[15]

Some people still push against this point by arguing that chance could yield the complex beauty of life if given enough time. Let's do a thought-experiment to test out that idea. Suppose you threw out blue, yellow, black, green, and red confetti from an airplane flying through the sky. What's the chance those bits of paper would fall to the ground and form a perfect Olympic flag, complete with five interlaced rings? Incredibly low—practically impossible. But let's follow the theory's logic and allow more time for the laws of nature to work on the confetti. Rain falls, disintegrating pieces of paper; wind blows, scattering confetti far out of sight; animals walk, trampling pieces as they go. Though all the necessary components are there, time does not increase the likelihood of a sophisticated design emerging from bits of paper.

In 1802, William Paley made famous what is known as "the watchmaker analogy." The premise is simple: "If we found a watch on the ground, its complexity would convince us that the watch did not occur naturally but was designed. Since both we and our universe are infinitely more complex than the watch, logic demands an eternal 'Watchmaker' who could have designed both us and our world."[16] There are many things in our world that, though amazing, can be explained easily enough by time and external forces. The Grand Canyon is a stunning example. While breathtaking in its beauty, the canyon is the result of erosion working over centuries; there's not a greater design there. In contrast, the pyramids of Egypt were clearly not formed through erosion or other natural forces. Intelligent people built them. We can find advanced patterns throughout nature, built into the very configuration of the everyday objects that make up our world—from the symmetry of a plant's leaves to the spirals of a snail's shell to the tessellation of the honeycomb. These aspects of nature are more intentional than random—more like the pyramids and less like the Grand Canyon.

The precision of these aspects of nature can't be explained merely by time and external forces. In fact, much of our world is so multifaceted, so extraordinarily intricate, that it becomes nearly impossible to conceive that all this occurred by chance. Like the inner workings of a watch, the beautiful complexity of our world compels us to consider the very real possibility that our world was purposefully designed. And, as William Paley wrote, "There cannot be a design without a designer."[17]

The Language of Life

In fact, scientific advances over the last few decades have revealed more and more just how extraordinary our world is. Take DNA, for example. We now know, thanks in large part to major discoveries in 1869 and 1953, that DNA molecules carry genetic instructions for the development, function, and reproduction of all known living organisms.[18] DNA molecules are made up of nucleotides, which each contain a nitrogen base. There are four potential nitrogen bases, and these bases bond together to form base pairs, the order of which determines the DNA's "instructions"—its genetic code. The cumulative DNA within our bodies forms our genome. You can think of DNA as the language of life and the human genome as the comprehensive instruction booklet that tells your body how to function. Within the human genome, the DNA code is *three billion* letters long.[19]

The exceedingly intricate composition of our bodies is mind-boggling, and the implications of that fact haven't gone unnoticed. In 2004, Antony Flew—a British philosopher, an Oxford professor, and an atheist since the age of fifteen—shocked the world when he declared his conversion to theism. Throughout his life, Flew endeavored to adhere to the Socratic principle that one "must follow the argument wherever it leads."[20] After studying the advances in DNA code and grappling with their significance, Flew concluded, "A super-intelligence is the only good explanation for the origin of life and the complexity of nature."[21] In his book *There Is a God: How the World's Most Notorious Atheist Changed His Mind*, Flew writes:

What I think the DNA material has done is that it has shown, by the almost unbeliev-able complexity of the arrangements which are needed to produce (life), that intelligence must have been involved in getting these extraordinarily diverse elements to work together. It's the enormous complexity of

---

Christians do not have a monopoly on morality.

---

the number of elements and the enormous subtlety of the ways they work together. The meeting of these two parts at the right time by chance is simply minute. It is all a matter of the enormous complexity by which the results were achieved, which looked to me like the work of intelligence.[22]

The Anthropic Principle

Like Flew, I am amazed by the complexity of our bodies. What's equally astounding is how exquisitely this world supports our existence. Scientists in multiple disciplines, from astronomy to microbiology, are seeing indications of the anthropic principle. The anthropic principle is the idea that the universe must have precise properties and conditions that either allow for or make inevitable the existence of conscious, sapient (that is, able to reason) beings like us. It seems that the universe was made specifically to support human life. The number of conditions that happen to be *exactly* right—"exactly" in the sense that the slightest variation would result in the impossibility of human life—is truly astonishing.

Gravity, electromagnetism, nuclear force, and the cosmological constant all operate within extremely narrow parameters. If they shifted in the slightest degree, the universe would either fly apart or collapse on itself. Proton size, the color of the sun, the ratio of gases in our atmosphere . . . the list of "just right" factors goes on and on. As environmental scientist Bob Davis put it, "The sheer *degree* of precision is hard to fathom. It would be equivalent to a recipe requiring us to count individual grains of sugar, measure molecules of milk, and calculate to the thousandths of a degree the temperature of the oven and the correct fraction of a second for it to shut off."[23]

Take a moment to consider the sheer wonder of birth or the marvel of our human senses. What about the ability to love, to feel, to imagine, to create, to appreciate beauty? Some say it takes more faith to believe all of this came about by chance than to believe our world—and those living in it—are custom-designed. I can't help but agree with astronomer Allan Sandage, who said, "I find it quite improbable that such order came out of chaos. There has to be some organizing principle. God to me is a mystery but is the explanation for the miracle of existence, why there is something instead of nothing."[24]

Candle #3: Morality

Let's turn our attention to the third candle lighting

our exploration of God's existence: morality. Most of us have an innate sense of right and wrong, a feeling that there are certain ways we should and shouldn't act. The most comprehensive moral is summed up in what is often called the Golden Rule: treat others the way you want to be treated.[25] You can find variations of the Golden Rule in most major religions and philosophies, from ancient Egypt (likely predating the Bible) to India, China, and Persia. Within social psychology, the reciprocity principle echoes this sentiment; as a social norm, we pay back what we receive from others. If someone does something for us, we feel compelled to return the favor.

Before we go on, let's clear up something right out of the gate: Christians do not have a monopoly on morality. Many atheists lead incredibly moral lives, fighting for social justice, equality, and fairness. The same goes for agnostics, Muslims, Buddhists, Hindus, Jews, and countless others. Morality is universal; it crosses all the barriers we humans have erected, whether religious, economic, or geographic.

This doesn't mean we all share the same moral code. Legislation varies vastly throughout the world. Laws differ on the legality of marijuana and alcohol, details of property ownership, women's rights, and endless other issues. But we all recognize that genocide is wrong. It's not a matter of opinion. We know there is a moral difference between Mother Teresa and Adolf Hitler. Consider our human experiences of guilt and shame; we know when we've done wrong. We give apologies and we ask forgiveness and we make amends.

The Truth and Reconciliation Commission was created to help repair the devastation of apartheid and genocide in South Africa, and similar initiatives have taken place in other countries.[26] Recovery programs like Alcoholics Anonymous include making amends as one of the steps to recovery. The need to reconcile broken relationships reveals the existence of morality.

A Morals Maker

Morality is fascinating when you stop to think about it. Though there are divergences, the majority of cultures throughout history have agreed upon certain constructs: avoid violence against your neighbor whenever possible; don't take what's not yours; tell the truth. Murder, theft, and lying are frowned upon worldwide, and they have been for eons. Of course, that doesn't mean everyone always acts within these moral boundaries—we all know that. In fact, our sense of morality is perhaps most clearly demonstrated in our reactions to others "crossing the line." When someone steals from you or lies to you, you react strongly and instinctively. You're angry; you feel betrayed. You know you've been wronged.

So we know morality exists, but why does it? Where did this pervasive sense of morality come from—what is its original source? How did we, as a collective, decide that some things were right, just, and good . . . and some weren't? Why do we even care what anyone else does? But we did, and we do.

As we discussed earlier in this chapter, something cannot come from nothing. Morality didn't spring into existence out of thin air and somehow work itself into the hearts of billions of people across millennia. The drive for survival doesn't account for altruistic morality outside of the family group. The very existence and universality of morals seem to imply a morals maker. Because of the reality of morality, the majority of theists (crossing a variety of religions and worldviews) believe that a sense of right and wrong was put into the hearts of humans by a divine being.

Candle #4: Experience

Our fourth candle brings the light of millions of personal testimonies. While this component is very different from a scientific discipline, it can't be ignored. In diverse cultures in every civilization since the beginning of history, people have sensed the direction of a higher power in their lives, have experienced supernatural strength empowering them for a difficult task, and have seen answers to their prayers. Lives have been changed.

It's certainly possible for a deluded or deceitful person to manufacture a claim to religious experience; we know that these things happen from time to time. But we're not talking about one or two people; we're not even talking about hundreds or thousands of people. Across the world over millennia, countless people—including some of the best and finest thinkers—have testified to having real experiences with a higher power. Scientists, doctors, business leaders, tech developers, teachers, artists, mothers, fathers, children—people from every walk of life bear witness to feeling the presence and even the love of God. They claim to have received forgiveness from God. They say their lives have been changed for the better by their encounters with God. They say they know God is real because they have met him.

But so what, right? Someone saying something doesn't make it true. Yet the number of people sharing these experiences is too overwhelming to ignore or simply write off. The testimony of millions

---

The strongest faiths are those forged and refined through the process of gathering, examining, and analyzing the evidence.

---

across sociological and cultural strata invites further consideration. Could all of these people be hallucinating or lying? Could they all be self-deceived? Can this be dismissed as an elaborate, worldwide, transhistorical conspiracy? Sure. Anything is possible. But there's no denying that it's a pretty big stretch. If even one person is telling the truth about an experience with God, then it becomes increasingly difficult to dismiss the idea of God altogether. It makes sense to consider the very real possibility that God exists.

Getting Personal

Think back through your life. Perhaps you've had an experience that seemed almost supernatural. Something aligned too perfectly to be just coincidence.

Something worked out just the way you needed it to in the nick of time. A seemingly irredeemable situation turned into something beautiful. The longer I live, the more experiences with God I have. In some of the most difficult moments of my life, I've sensed God's presence and felt a supernatural peace come over me; I have no other way to describe it. In times when I felt lost and didn't know where to turn, I have seen my desperate prayers answered.

My personal experience points to God's existence and fortifies my faith. My voice is one more added to a chorus that's been sung for millennia. Against the background of human diversity, any commonality found is compelling. The isolated experience of one person counts for only so much, but a common thread woven throughout the tapestry of human history has much more significance. Taken as a whole, personal testimony is a strong, bright candle with which to light our room.

A Well-Lit Room

Let's return to ancient Athens. As the Apostle Paul brought his speech to a close, he dropped the biggest bombshell yet: Jesus's resurrection from the dead. This, Paul contended, was proof of God's existence and his plan for all humankind.[27] Well, you can imagine the reaction that drew. Even if they could agree that the one true God existed, many in Athens were not at all ready to consider Jesus as God. After Paul finished speaking, the Athenians reacted in three different ways: some sneered; some said they'd like to hear Paul speak again; some believed. That is, some dismissed what Paul said; some put off making a decision one way or another; some accepted what Paul said as truth. We see this same range of responses today.

As we've just discussed, belief in God's existence is not an abandonment of intellectual honesty. A strong belief can be based on the carefully considered evidence of logic, science, morality, and experience. But facts can be interpreted in different ways, as was demonstrated by Paul's audience in Athens. No one can be forced to believe or disbelieve something. Rather, the strongest faiths are those forged and refined through the process of gathering, examining, and analyzing the evidence. Remember, realizations uncovered on one's own terms are the ones that have the potential to truly transform us.

The lines of evidence we've explored do not validate Christianity or any other religion. They simply point to the existence of God. For millions of people, including myself, these four candles bring enough light to see that God exists. But there is one major counterargument that we haven't talked about yet. It's great to recall my wonderful experiences in the Rocky Mountains, but what about those who have been killed by natural disasters in the midst of that very beauty? Why do we experience death and sickness and sadness? If God is real, why doesn't he put a stop to genocide, rape, and terrorism? How could a good God allow all that to happen? If there is a God, why is there pain and suffering in the world?

Endnotes for Chapter 2

1. A. W. Tozer, *The Knowledge of the Holy* (New York: HarperCollins, 1978), 1.

2. C. S. Lewis, *The Weight of Glory* (New York: HarperCollins, 2001), 38. First published 1941.

3. *The Holy Bible*, New International Version © 2011, Acts 17:16.

4. *The Holy Bible*, Acts 17:23.

5. *The Holy Bible*, Acts 17:23.

6. Gabe Bullard, "The World's Newest Major Religion: No Religion," *National Geographic*, April 22, 2016.

7. You can read Paul's speech in *The Holy Bible*, Acts 17:22–34.

8. For more information, see "Cosmological Argument," *Stanford Encyclopedia of Philosophy*, last modified October 11, 2017, https://plato.stanford.edu/entries/cosmological-argument/.

9. Richard Rogers, "Something Good," *The Sound of Music*, RCA Victor, 1965.

10. For example, Copernicus, Kepler, Pascal, Galileo, Faraday, and Newton are some of the most celebrated scientists in history. All were theists. Robert Boyle, the founder of modern chemistry, even suggested that the study of science would only increase the wonder at God's ordering of creation.

11. Albert Einstein, "Science and Religion," *Out of My Later Years* (New York: Philosophical Library, 1950).

12. For more information, refer to Alvin Plantinga, *Where the Conflict Really Lies: Science, Religion, and Naturalism* (Oxford University Press, 2018). Plantinga argues that it is naturalism and science (not religion and science) that are ultimately incompatible.

13. Charles Darwin to botanist Joseph Hooker, 1871. Full quote available in David C. Katling, *Astrobiology: A Very Short Introduction* (Oxford University Press, 2013)

14. Fred Hoyle and Chandra Wickramasinghe, *Evolution from Space: A Theory of Cosmic Creationism* (New York: Simon & Schuster, 1984).

15. Fred Hoyle, "Hoyle on Evolution," *Nature* 294, no. 5837 (November 12, 1981): 105.

16. Louis Markos, PhD, "Chance, Evolution, or Intelligent Design?" *Explore God*, http://www.exploregod.com/chance-evolution-or-intelligent-design.

17. William Paley, *Natural Theology*, ed. Frederick Ferré (New York: Bobbs-Merrill, 1963), 3–6.

18. Friedrich Miescher first isolated what are now known as nucleic acids in 1869. In 1953, James Watson and Francis Crick discovered the structure of the DNA molecule, which paved the way to understanding how DNA communicates genetic information.

19. Francis S. Collins, *The Language of God* (New York: Free Press, 2006), 1.

20. Antony Flew and Roy Abraham Varghese, *There Is a God: How the World's Most Notorious Atheist Changed His Mind* (New York: Harper Collins, 2007), 23.

21. Antony Flew, telephone interview, *ABC News*, ABC, December 9, 2004.

22. *Flew and Varghese*, 74.

23. Bob Davis, "When Mere Coincidence Fails to Explain," Explore God, https://www.exploregod.com/articles/when-mere-coincidence-fails-to-explain.

24. J. N. Willford, "Sizing Up the Cosmos: An Astronomers Quest," *New York Times*, March 12, 1991, B9.

25. *The Holy Bible*, Matthew 7:12.

26. For more information, see Onur Bakiner, *Truth Commissions: Memory, Power, and Legitimacy* (Philadelphia: University of Pennsylvania Press, 2015).

27. *The Holy Bible*, Acts 17:31.

CHAPTER THREE

Why Does God Allow Pain and Suffering?

"I hurt myself today to see if I still feel. I focus on the pain, the only thing that's real." —"Hurt," Nine Inch Nails[1]

My friend's little boy was playing outside near the family truck one day when somehow the brake released and the truck rolled down the driveway, crushing the boy to death. He was three years old. You may be shaking your head in dismay right now as you read this and asking yourself, *Why did that happen?* Why did that little boy die? Why did that family have to endure such heartbreak? If there is a God, why didn't he stop that truck?

There have always been challenges that come with being a pastor. Caring for those who have lost (or are actively losing) loved ones is high on the list. But during the height of the pandemic, it was particularly excruciating. When one of our beloved staff members got COVID-19, his family wasn't allowed into his hospital room. When he passed away, still his wife and children could not be with him. So I met his family not in a private room but on a concrete sidewalk outside the building. We stood—six feet away from each other—in full public view of everyone coming and going. His wife and children sobbed in the cold as the sun went down until they finally had to leave. I've seen a lot of loss. But I've never seen despair like that.

Why, why, why?

It's a natural, instinctual, unavoidable response. I asked those very questions. We don't understand why these things happen. If you're like me, sometimes you may doubt there is a reason at all. Sometimes it feels like the only thing you do know for sure is that you're hurting. You don't know why you're suffering or when it will end—you just know that you're in pain. On any given day, world news inundates us with stories of tragedy, despair, and hopelessness: wildfires destroy hundreds of homes, earthquakes displace thousands of people, wars rip apart nations and families, millions struggle to survive every day. We read of, see, or experience injustice, oppression, and exploitation daily. And when tragedy strikes in our lives or the lives of those we love, it's nothing short of agony.

Over the last two years, the world has mourned much. The sheer amount of suffering has been overwhelming, even paralyzing. If you believe in a higher power, these feelings can often give way to deeper questions: Why are you punishing me, God? How could you let this happen to us? Why didn't you prevent this? From there, it's natural to follow our human logic to a darker place: Maybe God isn't a loving figure after all. Maybe God doesn't care what happens to any of us. Maybe God himself is evil. Thoughts like these lead people to sympathize with atheist Richard Dawkins's characterization of God as:

> Arguably the most unpleasant character in all fiction: jealous and proud of it; a petty, unjust, unforgiving control-freak; a vindictive, bloodthirsty ethnic cleanser; a misogynistic, homophobic, racist, infanticidal, genocidal, filicidal, pestilential, megalomaniacal, sadoma-sochistic, capriciously malevolent bully.[2]

Brutal. If God is like that—if God sees all the evil happening down here and ignores it (or worse, makes it happen)—frankly, I want nothing to do with him. Why would I? Why would anyone? And yet billions of people not only believe in God, but talk to him, worship him, and seek out his will for their lives. How do they reconcile their belief in a good, all-powerful God with the very real presence of evil in this world—and lots of it?

Acknowledging Pain and Suffering

A few years ago, our twenty-nine-year-old son called to say he was feeling a tingling from the waist up. At first, he ignored it, but it just got worse. The tingling turned into numbness and then a completely debilitating loss of feeling in most of his body. The doctors found nothing, and the symptoms worsened. The possibilities terrified us. Our son who rode mountain bikes, snowboarded down black-diamond courses, and raced in triathlons could barely hold a fork to feed himself. One morning he called and said, with a catch in his voice, "Dad, they figured it out. I have multiple sclerosis—MS." I was stunned. While we talked, I held it together, but when I hung up the phone, I sobbed. I knew nothing would ever be the same. MS is chronic, and it can be incapacitating. Why *my* son? He hadn't done anything wrong. He was a good kid. He is a good man. *Why, God?*

No rational theorizing can heal a broken heart. No philosophical discussion can comfort a torn soul aching from a devastating loss. We've all been broken in one way or another; we've had the breath knocked out of us by hard hits, whether physical or emotional. Every person carries private hurts. They may not be as obvious as my son's symptoms, but they're every bit as real. My heart aches for the suffering in our world. I ache for those struggling with depression and anxiety, continually fighting against the darkness. I ache for the men, women, and children who live with the trauma of verbal, physical, and sexual abuse. I ache for the abandoned, neglected, and forgotten. I ache for those who mourn friends and family; who lost graduations, weddings, and celebrations; who face the continuing impact of the collective trauma of the pandemic. I'm sorry—truly, deeply sorry. I wish I could fix all of it. I wish none of it ever happened.

It's heartless to minimize another person's pain,

either by dismissing it or by settling for greeting-card sentiments and sympathies. You may be in a bad place right now, wrestling with how God could allow so much darkness in our world. You may be so devastated that you see no option but to reject the idea of God entirely. That's understandable. The presence of pain and suffering in our lives is perhaps the most significant challenge to faith in an omnipotent, benevolent God.

Explaining Pain and Suffering

Human attempts to explain evil, pain, and suffering can be traced back through millennia. In fact, we can even read three- to four-thousand-year-old stories to see their explanations for why bad things happen.[3] Every philosophy, religion, and worldview wrestles with how to make sense of pain and suffering and how to offer some hope in the midst of it. While no theory or explanation can fully remove the sting of grief and pain, there are three common approaches to answering the question of pain and suffering. For the sake of simplification, let's call them optimism, pessimism, and dualism.

The optimistic view could go a couple of ways. The Buddhist philosophy, for example, says that our world—and the pain and suffering therein—is just an illusion. Buddhists believe that human desires cause all suffering; as such, suffering can be eliminated by removing human desires and achieving enlightenment. Enlightenment breaks the illusion that our world, pain, and suffering are real. Another optimistic perspective says that what appears to be evil is actually good. If you could just see the big picture, you'd see the good in every seemingly bad thing; all suffering leads to a greater good. This optimist will point out that we learn more from failure than success and that pain teaches us lessons we could never learn otherwise. There is truth in this view, but it seems to downplay or even dismiss the reality of our pain.

The pessimist says we shouldn't be surprised when misfortune befalls us, because pain and suffering are just reality. You live, you hurt, you die. It's harsh, but it's the way the world works. Sometimes this view comes from a place of scientific naturalism; a person with this perspective may point to the survival of the fittest as an example. Pain is part of the natural order of things and serves no higher purpose. Some nihilist philosophers, who believe that existence is senseless and useless, go one step further. Not only is suffering just the state of things, but we also can't even claim that pain is bad, because we have no moral basis on which to make such a judgment. It's true that none of us can ever fully understand the reasons for suffering, but this view leaves us with a sense of purposelessness and despair.

Dualists say that good and evil are two equal forces that have been in conflict for all eternity. Pain and suffering are the results of this battle. Historically, this view is found in Manichaeism, a religious movement that taught of a cosmic struggle between the spiritual world of good and light and the material world of evil and darkness. The dualist view gives us some great works of literature and film; you can think of it as the

Star Wars philosophy. In these stories, we often see a force for evil and a force for good battling to rule the universe.

Reconciling God and Evil

But where does God fit in any of this? In the Christian view, God recognizes the presence of evil in the world; it's not an illusion but a disturbing reality. And while painful circumstances can sometimes lead to beautiful results, evil is never good in itself. We've all gone through rough times that turned out to be for the best, but that doesn't change the fact that evil is evil. Furthermore, Christians believe there is no force equal to God, so there can't be two equal forces at war with each other. Rather, there is only one omnipotent being, and that is God.

This last point has often compelled people to ask the obvious follow-up question: If God is all-good (omnibenevolent) and all-powerful (omnipotent), with none to equal him, then why do bad things happen? Epicurus, a Greek philosopher born in 341 BCE, is generally credited with first summing up this issue in the Epicurean paradox:

> Is God willing to prevent evil, but not able? Then he is not omnipotent. Is he able, but not willing? Then he is malevolent. Is he both able and willing? Then whence cometh evil? Is he neither able nor willing? Then why call him God?[4]

Over the centuries since Epicurus lived, theologians have taken several approaches to resolve this assumed dissonance—the "problem of evil," as it is sometimes identified. These attempts are called theodicies. Theodicies work not only to show that the existence of evil doesn't preclude God's existence but also to provide a framework for understanding how a good, all-powerful God can allow evil to persist in the world. Knowing how these theodicies have been informed by the Bible can help us understand the theodicies themselves.

Put most simply, the Bible is a story of how the world came to be, what has gone wrong in the world, and what God is doing to set the world right again. Within the biblical worldview, pain is neither permanent nor intrinsically necessary. Rather, it is the result of human failings—of sin, brokenness, and selfishness. Though this isn't always the most popular standpoint (understandably, no one likes to be blamed for anything), it does mean that a biblical view of suffering is uniquely linear. Pain has not always existed, and it will not always exist; there was a beginning, and there will be an end. These experiences are just one chapter in the story of our world. Let's take a look at that story arc in the context of three acts, which we'll call Creation, Fall, and Salvation.

Creation: God Creates Good Things

Let's start at the beginning, which is usually the best place to start, don't you think? For Christians and

Jews alike, the beginning is found in the book of Genesis— even the word "genesis" means "origin" or "beginning." In the very first verse of the first chapter of the Bible, we read, "In the beginning, God created the heavens and the earth."[5] After this, God goes on to create light and darkness; the sky, water, and land; the sun, moon, and stars; and plants, animals, and humans.[6] After each step, we read, "And God saw that

---

If you took all the good things out of the world, there would be nothing left. Evil would not remain in its place, because evil cannot exist on its own.

---

it was good."[7] The Apostle Paul, whom we talked about in our last chapter, explained simply, "Everything God created is good."[8]

Within Christianity, God's character is known to be entirely good, without any darkness or evil in it.[9] And yet, pain, suffering, tragedy, misfortune, wickedness, and evil all exist. You may have noticed that our list above didn't mention God creating any of those things. So how can we reconcile the belief that God is good and created "all things" with the existence of evil?[10] Where did evil come from?

If you grew up in church, you might say evil came from Satan. That's a fair response. But then who created Satan? Quite simply, God did. But there's a caveat: As we just discussed, God created everything to be good. Every part of creation—including the devil—

was originally "very good."[11] In fact, many Christians believe that Satan was originally created as an angel to serve and glorify God. The Bible indicates that at some point before our world existed, a group of angels rebelled against God.[12] Based on Scripture, it seems likely that Satan led this heavenly revolt.[13] As a result, many Christians see Satan as the first sinner; he "has been sinning from the beginning."[14] Jesus himself calls the devil "a murderer from the beginning. . . . the father of lies."[15]

But does this mean that Satan is the source of evil? Or is God the source because he created Satan, from whom evil arose? Some people believe the answer is simple: if God created everything in the world and evil is something in the world, then God must have created evil. This seems to follow solid logic. But I agree with many thinkers throughout history who suggest there is a flaw in the second part of this statement. Evil is not "something in the world" but rather a *lack* of something else.

Evil as the Absence of Good

According to many theologians and philosophers, evil is not a thing itself. Augustine, a theologian and philosopher who lived from 354 to 430CE, described evil as the absence of good. Augustine wrote:

> For what is that which we call evil but the absence of good? In the bodies of animals, disease and wounds mean nothing but the absence of health; for when a cure is effect-ed, that does not mean

that the evils which were present—namely, the diseases and wounds—go away from the body and dwell elsewhere: they altogether cease to exist; for the wound or disease is not a substance, but a defect in the fleshly substance,—the flesh itself being a substance, and therefore something good, of which those evils—that is, privations of the good which we call health—are accidents. Just in the same way, what are called vices in the soul are nothing but privations of natural good. And when they are cured, they are not transferred elsewhere: when they cease to exist in the healthy soul, they cannot exist anywhere else.[16]

This understanding of evil is not unique to Christianity. You can see this worldview in a variety of religions and philosophies, from the Neoplatonists to followers of the Bahá'í Faith. 'Abdu'l-Bahá, the son of the founder of the Bahá'í Faith, has written:

It is possible that one thing in relation to another may be evil, and at the same time within the limits of its proper being it may not be evil. Then it is proved that there is no evil in existence; all that God created He created good. This evil is nothingness; so death is the absence of life. When man no longer receives life, he dies. Darkness is the absence of light: when there is no light, there is darkness. Light is an existing thing, but darkness is nonexistent.[17]

Ponder this thought: If you took all the good things out of the world, there would be nothing left. Evil would not remain in its place, because evil cannot exist on its own.

Free Will and Responsibility

As we continue in Genesis, we learn that "God created mankind in his own image."[18] As God has the freedom to act, so—albeit in a much more limited way—do humans have the freedom to make choices. With this freedom comes responsibility; as your parents always told you, choices come with consequences. People can choose love, righteousness, and justice. We equally can choose hate, immorality, and inequity.

One of the most compelling and influential responses to the issue of evil is Augustine's "free-will theodicy." Augustine taught that evil exists as a necessary possibility in a world of free, morally conscious beings. From this perspective, a world without any possibility of pain would be a world without any possibility of free choice or true love—a world full of automatons, not real human beings. But God gave people the gift and responsibility of choice, the ability to give our love freely to another. Forced love is not love at all. If I coerced or bribed my granddaughter to give me a hug, it would mean little. But when my granddaughter wraps her little arms around my neck and gives me a big kiss, my joy is sweet because I know she chose to give me her love. When we choose to volunteer, donate our resources, or show up in times of crisis for people we don't even know, that's love in action. And that love is being given freely, voluntarily, of our own volition.

Yes, God could have created a world of robots unable to hurt each other, a universe of puppets without an independent thought in their heads. But imagine what we would lose as humans if all our choices were removed, if we had no ability to make decisions with consequences. We would be reduced to automatons. Instead, our world contains opportunities for moral choices and love as well as immoral choices and hate. Every day, each one of us is free to make choices that carry real consequences. Sometimes we choose wisely; other times we hurt others and ourselves.

Fall: God Grieves Our Pain

The first evidence of human choice comes very early in the story of our existence, in the form of Adam and Eve's reaction to an instruction from God. After creating man and woman, God told them, "You are free to eat from any tree in the garden; but you must not eat from the tree of the knowledge of good and evil, for when you eat from it you will certainly die."[19] Adam and Eve had a choice of what to do with God's commandment. They could do as he said, or they could defy his instruction and eat from the tree. People have choices, and actions have far-reaching consequences—sometimes more so than we ever thought possible.

Decisions Have Consequences

The next portion of Genesis tells the story of what

is commonly known as "the Fall"—Adam and Eve's decision to disobey God. "When the woman saw that the fruit of the tree was good for food and pleasing to the eye, and also desirable for gaining wisdom, she took some and ate it. She also gave some to her husband, who was with her, and he ate it."[20] This action—often called "original sin"—had devastating ramifications. The consequences were swift and brutal:

> To the woman [God] said, "I will make your pains in childbearing very severe; with painful labor you will give birth to children. Your desire will be for your husband, and he will rule over you." To Adam he said, "Because you listened to your wife and ate fruit from the tree about which I commanded you, 'You must not eat from it,' "Cursed is the ground because of you; through painful toil you will eat food from it all the days of your life. It will produce thorns and thistles for you, and you will eat the plants of the field. By the sweat of your brow you will eat your food until you return to the ground, since from it you were taken; for dust you are and to dust you will return." . . . So the Lord God banished him from the Garden of Eden to work the ground from which he had been taken.[21]

Does that seem like kind of an overreaction on God's part? I can certainly understand that perspective. But though eating the fruit was a seemingly small act, through their choice to do so, Adam and Eve rebelled against God on a profound level. By choosing to defy

God, they not only disregarded God's command but also doubted his goodness and challenged his authority. They thought God was keeping something from them that they deserved to have, and they decided that they knew what was best for them, better than God did.

As the founders of humanity, Adam and Eve's decision caused inestimable damage to the human race and the planet. It may not seem fair that all of humanity should have to suffer because of a mistake someone else made millennia ago. But Christians believe that, similarly to how we inherit physical traits from our parents, we also inherit spiritual characteristics. In this way, having a sinful nature is a matter of what you could consider our "spiritual genetics." Here, the theological concept of federal headship comes into play. Federal headship may seem like an intimidating phrase but in essence it means simply that, as the first created human, Adam was the "head" of the human race, representing all humanity. And his actions (like his choice to disobey God) represented the actions of all humanity. We see something similar when a parent's actions impact the entire family. The Bible explains it this way: "sin entered the world through one man, and death through sin, and in this way death came to all people, because all sinned."[22]

Indeed, since that day in the garden, we have followed in Adam's footsteps through our sinful behavior. After their banishment from Eden, Adam and Eve had two sons, Cain and Abel. As time went on, Cain grew jealous of Abel, eventually killing him out of anger. Jews, Christians, and Muslims alike regard this act as the first murder committed on earth. As a result, we are "sinners twice over: we sin because we are sinners (Adam's choice), and we are sinners because we sin (our choice). . . . We are more than *potential* sinners; we are *practicing* sinners."[23]

Disobedience entered the picture, and with it came shame, brokenness, and eventual death, just as God said it would. The evil that entered our world affected nature, too. As we read earlier, even the earth itself was cursed as a result of Adam and Eve's choice. Many believe this to be the root cause of natural disasters. While science thoroughly explains *how* these events occur, it does not necessarily provide a satisfactory answer to the question of *why*. Why do we have hurricanes, floods, tornadoes, droughts, and earthquakes? Many Christians believe that the pain that comes from these events ultimately arises as a result of the curse on the ground. The original human couple sinned, and our whole world was affected. Sin almost always impacts those around us; in this case, the reach of original sin is still being felt.

Did God care about any of this? Does he care that we're hurting? How did the entrance of evil into the world affect God?

Our Pain Causes God Pain

For most of us, it's natural to grieve when someone is hurting, just as I mourned with my friend over the loss of his son. Most of us also condemn evil acts, like when someone mistreats or abuses someone else. But perhaps the scariest times are those when we glimpse into our own souls and see the evil there—the pettiness, the hatefulness, the bitterness. Most of the time we don't allow ourselves to see our own evil; it's uncomfortable and shameful to face the darkness in our hearts . . . but it's real nonetheless.

I get so frustrated with myself when I mess up, and I feel horrible when I cause someone pain with my selfishness or unkind words. I grieve when my actions hurt those around me. We have to tackle the ugliness in our hearts and in our world head-on. We should grieve abuse, senseless violence, and injustice. We should grieve inequality, hatred, and every time self-interest wins out over compassion.

Genesis 6 tells us that grief is precisely what God felt when evil came into the world: "The Lord saw how great the wickedness of the human race had become on the earth, and that every inclination of the thoughts of

---

For Christians, the crucifixion is paradoxically the darkest and brightest moment in all world history.

---

the human heart was only evil all the time. The Lord regretted that he had made human beings on the earth, and his heart was deeply troubled."[24] God's heart was full of pain when he saw the evil in his world.

Think of how hard it is to see those whom you love make mistakes, cause others pain, and hurt themselves. Christians believe it's the same for God; in fact, from the Christian perspective, the heartache God feels over the pain we cause each other and the evil in the world is even greater than we can understand. God knows the world was not meant to be this way—we were not made to oppress, violate, and kill each other. Yet our capacity for evil seems to know no bounds. The world is broken, and God's heart breaks for it.

But if God is so disturbed by the state of the world, why doesn't he do something about it?

Salvation: God Saves Us from Our Pain and Suffering

In the centuries after the Fall, things on this earth deteriorated terribly. We read that the world and the human race grew corrupt and became filled with violence. God could have totally destroyed the world he made, and he would have been justified. But instead, God did something very, very different. Here's a preview of what we'll dive into more in chapter 5: according to the Christian understanding, in his unfathomable, limitless love, God took the drastic step of becoming human in order to take upon himself the evil in the world. Jesus came into the world fully God and fully human.

He lived a perfect life, died on the cross for our sins, bore the burden of our shortcomings, and then rose from the grave—defeating sin, brokenness, and death. Sin came into the world through Adam and Eve's free choice, and it was overcome through Jesus's free choice. Just as Adam and Eve chose to disobey God, incurring death through sin, so Jesus Christ chose to die for us, conquering death through resurrection. In the Christian understanding, Jesus committed the ultimate act of love so that he might save us from suffering and evil.

The cross is crucial to Christianity. The cross of Jesus Christ is what God did against evil. Christians understand Jesus to be the fulfillment of the words recorded by the prophet Isaiah centuries before Jesus was born:

> Surely he took up our pain and bore our suffering, yet we considered him punished by God, stricken by him, and afflicted. But he was pierced for our transgressions, he was crushed for our iniquities; the punishment that brought us peace was on him, and by his wounds we are healed. We all, like sheep, have gone astray, each of us has turned to our own way; and the Lord has laid on him the iniquity of us all.[25]

Jesus Christ took on the sorrows and sins of all humankind and carried them to the cross. There he experienced all the despair, desperation, and isolation of an entire species separated from God. He suffered and died so that we might find forgiveness for our sins, salvation from ourselves, and reconciliation with God. For Christians, the crucifixion is paradoxically the darkest and brightest moment in all world history. In her book *Letters to a Diminished Church*, Dorothy Sayers writes:

> For whatever reason God chose to make people as they are—limited and suffering and subject to sorrows and death—he had the honesty and

courage to take his own medicine. Whatever game he is playing with his creation, he has kept his own rules and played fair. He can exact nothing from us that he has not exacted from himself. He has himself gone through the whole human experience, from the trivial irritations of family life and the cramping restrictions of hard work and lack of money to the worst horrors of pain and humiliation, defeat, despair, and death. When he was man, he played the man. He was born in poverty and died in disgrace and thought it all worthwhile.[26]

God Will End Our Pain and Suffering

The Christian faith says that the resurrection isn't the end of the story. One day, Christ will return. All evil and pain will be eliminated, replaced with perfect peace and joy. Though the Bible never guarantees that our suffering will cease in this life, it concludes with the promise of a glorious future in which all pain and suffering will be gone forever: "Look! God's dwelling place is now among the people, and he will dwell with them. They will be his people, and God himself will be with them and be their God. He will wipe every tear from their eyes. There will be no more death or mourning or crying or pain, for the old order of things has passed away."[27]

According to the Bible, whatever horrible evil you have experienced, whatever pain is paralyzing you, will one day be taken away.[28] "The image of God wiping away tears from the eyes of his people communicates not merely the *cessation of* earthly suffering, but *consolation for* earthly suffering."[29] Suffering is not the whole story of our world. The corruption of evil will be undone; beauty, peace, and goodness will be restored. Your tears of sorrow will become tears of joy.

Why Doesn't God End Evil Now?

That's a lovely picture, but still questions remain: Why doesn't God get rid of evil right now? Why let one more person be abused? Be diagnosed with cancer? Get killed in a drive-by shooting? Why let all this go on? These types of questions press especially hard when you're asking yourself and God why *you* lost your job, why *your* baby died, why *you* have chronic pain.

Trying to answer these questions may be comparable to trying to walk in shoes that are too big for us. Who's to say that God understands things the way we do? If we believe we're talking about a God who is big enough to create the entire universe—a God who created us, even—why would we expect our thoughts to be on the same level as God's thoughts? In fact, the Bible says outright that God's ways are not like ours: "'For my thoughts are not your thoughts, neither are your ways my ways,' declares the Lord. 'As the heavens are higher than the earth, so are my ways higher than your ways and my thoughts than your thoughts.'"[30] It's possible that we simply don't—and couldn't—comprehend the answers to our questions.

There is another factor to take into account as well. Consider the Apostle Peter's words: "The Lord is not slow in keeping his promise, as some understand slowness. Instead he is patient with you, not wanting anyone to perish, but everyone to come to repentance."[31] By allowing evil to survive in this world, God postpones the day of final judgment. Though it seems quite counterintuitive, consider the possibility that God allows evil to continue out of mercy. Were God to rid the world of evil now, according to the Christian faith, all who have yet to hear and accept the good news of Jesus Christ would be lost for eternity. No one else would enter God's kingdom. Perhaps in God's eyes, the "lesser evil" is to allow this temporary suffering to continue while millions who are lost are given more time to be found.

The truth is, none of us can say with certainty why evil is allowed to continue in this world. What we do know is that, according to the Bible, God is not the author of evil. God makes only good things. God grieves our pain and suffering. God came to earth as Jesus Christ to suffer and die for the forgiveness of our sins. God will end our pain and suffering one day. The biblical story of creation, fall, and salvation addresses the problem of evil intellectually, but those answers rarely bring comfort in the darkness of intense pain and suffering.

The Bible doesn't hide from this deep grief. In the midst of their agony, biblical characters like Job, Habakkuk, and Jeremiah screamed out their confusion over what God was doing in the world. The entire book of Lamentations is devoted to prayers of grief and sorrow; the author cries out over the pain in this world and our inability to understand it. In the book of Psalms, grief, despair, and lament are common themes. The Bible doesn't shy away from the reality of our pain. Even Jesus wept over death and the pain it brings.[32]

Of course, knowing that Jesus suffered doesn't take away our pain. But the suffering of Christ can give us hope during tough times because it offers us something stronger than suffering—the love of God, a "love that surpasses knowledge."[33] As Tim Keller explains:

> If we again ask the question, "Why does God allow evil and suffering to continue?" and we look at the cross of Jesus, we still do not know what the answer is. However, now we know what the answer isn't. It can't be that he doesn't love us. It can't be that he is indifferent or detached from our condition. God takes our misery and suffering so seriously that he was willing to take it on himself.[34]

How to Cope with Pain and Suffering

So what do we do when we're actively suffering in the present? What does any of this mean practically? Suffering can produce different results for different people, depending on their responses to their circumstances. The exact same painful experience can make one person bitter and cynical but make another person compassionate and kind. What makes the difference?

> One important aspect of the Bible's teaching is the call to persevere with integrity through suffering.

> The Apostle James taught that trials should be considered "pure joy" because they produce perseverance.[35] The Apostle Paul took the concept even further, saying that "suffering produces perseverance; perseverance, character; and character, hope."[36] The New Testament repeatedly calls Christians to stand up under unjust suffering, and even to rejoice in it in light of God's redemptive purposes.[37] Suffering can sweeten and deepen us. Suffering can poison and embitter us. We have a choice.[38]

Jewish psychologist Viktor Frankl spent years in a Nazi concentration camp during the Holocaust. After his release, Frankl wrote about his experiences and observations during that time. In his book *Man's Search for Meaning*, he wrote: "Everything can be taken from a man but one thing: the last of the human freedoms—to choose one's attitude in any given set of circumstances, to choose one's own way."[39]

We have all seen how good can come from bad situations. For example, over the years I've seen multiple people across various groups try to unite people to care for our community. But it's never worked or had any staying power—until COVID hit. In 2020, the City Manager of McKinney got together community leaders, including the mayor, police and fire chiefs, the superintendent, directors of nonprofits, pastors, and business owners. Together, we formed One Heart McKinney. We met together virtually every week, raising over $200,000 to encourage and care for our people with food and shelter. We saw the suffering taking place in our community, and we took action to acknowledge it and—to the best of our abilities—resolve it.

In March 2021, we gathered in person for the first time. We appointed a task force to create One Heart McKinney 2.0 with a new mission: to coordinate the whole community to maximize well-being in daily life and respond to and recover from any community crisis. We know from experience that none of this would have happened without the COVID crisis.

We can choose to respond to pain in light of how God responds to it. We should refuse to throw out platitudes and superficial sympathies. We should acknowledge the reality of suffering and empathize with others, entering into their pain with them as Jesus Christ did. We can walk with people in their pain and comfort them with our presence. We can find and share the deep hope that one day, there will be no more sorrow. Until that day, we should stand against injustice, "mourn with those who mourn,"[40] and find comfort in God's presence and in the love we can offer to each other.[41] This is the Christian approach to pain and suffering.

But is the Christian way the only right way?

Endnotes for Chapter 3

1. Trent Reznor, "Hurt," *The Downward Spiral*, A&M Studios, released April 17, 1995.
2. Richard Dawkins, *The God Delusion* (New York: Bantam Books, 2006), 51.
3. Andrew George, *The Epic of Gilgamesh* (New York: Penguin Books, 1999).
4. John Hospers, *An Introduction to Philosophical Analysis*, 3rd ed. (Abingdon-on-Thames, UK: Routledge, 1990), 310.

5. *The Holy Bible*, New International Version © 2011, Genesis 1:1.
6. See *The Holy Bible*, Genesis 1.
7. *The Holy Bible*, Genesis 1:10, 12, 18, 21, 25.
8. *The Holy Bible*, 1 Timothy 4:4.
9. *The Holy Bible*, 1 John 1:5.
10. *The Holy Bible*, Colossians 1:16-17, Romans 11:36, 1 Corinthians 8:6.
11. *The Holy Bible*, Genesis 1:31.
12. *The Holy Bible*, 2 Peter 2:4 and Jude 6.
13. It seems clear that the devil is the leader of the demonic forces. Scripture refers to him as "the evil one" (Matthew 13:19), "the ruler of this world" (John 12:31), "the god of this age" (2 Corinthians 4:4), and "the ruler of the kingdom of the air" (Ephesians 2:2).
14. The Holy Bible, 1 John 3:8.
15. Ibid., John 8:44.
16. Augustine, The Enchiridion, Addressed to Laurentius; Being a Treatise on Faith, Hope, and Love, trans. J. F. Shaw, 1883.
17. 'Abdu'l-Bahá, "74. The Nonexistence of Evil," *Some Answered Questions* (US Bahá'í Publishing Trust, 1990), 263-264.
18. *The Holy Bible*, Genesis 1:27.
19. *The Holy Bible*, Genesis 2:16-17.
20. *The Holy Bible*, Genesis 3:6.
21. *The Holy Bible*, Genesis 3:16-19, 23.
22. *The Holy Bible*, Romans 5:12.
23. "Why do I face the consequences of Adam's sin when I did not eat the fruit?" Got Questions, https://www.gotquestions.org/I-did-not-eat-the-fruit.html.
24. *The Holy Bible*, Genesis 6:5-6. Some Bible translations use the word "grieved" instead of "regretted."
25. *The Holy Bible*, Isaiah 53:4-6.
26. Dorothy Sayers, *Letters to a Diminished Church: Passionate Arguments for the Relevance of Christian Doctrine* (Nashville: Thomas Nelson, 2004), 2.
27. *The Holy Bible*, Revelation 21:3-4.
28. Romans 8:21 tells us that even "the creation itself will be liberated from its bondage to decay and brought" into the freedom and glory of the children of God." The curse on the ground will be lifted.
29. Gavin Ortlund, "A Deeper Look at What the Bible Says about Pain and Suffering," Explore God, https://www.exploregod.com/articles/a-deeper-look-at-what-the-bible-says-about-pain-and-suffering.
30. *The Holy Bible*, Isaiah 55:8-9.
31. *The Holy Bible*, 2 Peter 3:9.
32. *The Holy Bible*, John 11:35.
33. *The Holy Bible*, Ephesians 3:19.
34. Tim Keller, *The Reason for God: Belief in an Age of Skepticism* (New York: Dutton, 2008), 30.
35. *The Holy Bible*, James 1:2-4.

36. *The Holy Bible*, Romans 5:3-4.

37. *The Holy Bible*, 1 Peter 4:12-19.

38. Ortlund, "A Deeper Look at What the Bible Says about Pain and Suffering."

39. Viktor E. Frankl, *Man's Search for Meaning* (1946; reprinted, Boston: Beacon Press, 2006), 75.

40. *The Holy Bible*, Romans 12:15.

41. If you'd like to read more about the Christian perspective on living with suffering, check out Nicholas Wolterstorff's *Lament for a Son*.

CHAPTER FOUR

Is Christianity Too Narrow?

"Imagine there's no heaven. It's easy if you try.
No hell below us, above us only sky. Imagine all the people
living for today. Imagine there's no countries. It isn't hard to
do. Nothing to kill or die for, and no religion too.
Imagine all the people living life in peace. You may say
I'm a dreamer, but I'm not the only one."
—"Imagine," John Lennon[1]

Have you ever heard the standard advice not to discuss religion or politics at the dinner table? This sentiment stems from the natural human inclination to avoid discomfort. Conversations around both subjects can be tense, awkward, and downright confrontational. This is especially true when someone tells you that their way of thinking is the only right way—particularly if you don't agree with their beliefs! This kind of interaction can be annoying, frustrating, and offensive.

In part, this is why we tend to put a premium on tolerance, inclusivity, and acceptance. We lean heavily on sayings like, "Let's agree to disagree." "You do you," we say. "To each their own." Maybe you've seen shirts or bumper stickers emblazoned with the word "COEXIST" spelled out via symbols of various world religions and philosophies. At the root of these statements is a sincere desire to achieve a harmonious coexistence among people from diverse faiths. But there's an underlying message at play, a subtle but consistent subtext: Religious tolerance and sharing your faith in order to encourage followers of a different religion to change their beliefs are mutually exclusive. Religious tolerance means you should not claim that your religion is the only correct one.

As you can tell from the last chapter, Jesus Christ is central to the Christian understanding of God's place in pain and suffering. In fact, Christians believe Jesus is the only way to make sense of our world and enter into a relationship with God. But many have objected to this view, calling it narrow, intolerant, and arrogant. In a world increasingly focused on tolerance and acceptance, isn't Christianity too narrow? Have you ever wondered if Christianity really is the only true religion? Is Jesus the only way to God, or are Christians just being too exclusive?

Unfortunately, there are narrow-minded, bigoted Christians who say outrageous things and do despicable things, all in the name of Jesus—and they tend to get the most press. But no one wants to be judged by extremism. To address these questions fairly, we must look at Christianity in terms of what the Bible teaches without getting distracted by distortions.

Religious Diversity

In the last few decades, globalism and our shrinking world have brought ever-increasing religious diversity into the average person's life. Though the world has been full of diverse religions for millennia, people often lived in cultural bubbles before the Internet and global media. Increased immigration has led to greater cultural diversity in cities, workplaces, and neighborhoods around the world. Now more than ever, the diversity of our world is evident, splashed across personal newsfeeds and TV screens.

In 2013, an area in the Dallas suburb of Irving was ranked by a national real estate website as the most diverse neighborhood in America.[2] Where I live, just north of Dallas, we share life with Hindus, Buddhists, Muslims, Mormons, Sikhs, Jews, Bahá'ís, Zoroastrians, secularists, agnostics, and atheists. While we have Christian friends, our lives are filled with people from different faiths and worldviews. I hope the same goes for you; diversity enriches our lives in countless ways. It's great to get to know people with different traditions. But when you come to know and love people from other religions, the exclusivity of Christianity can become increasingly uncomfortable. Is it really necessary to say Jesus is the *only* way? Can't all religions be right?

Religious Pluralism

Some tackle this question from a pluralistic perspective. Consider this oft-repeated illustration: God is seated at the top of a mountain. There are many paths to reach the peak, where God can be found. On one side of the mountain is Christianity; on another is Islam. Hinduism is yet another path. Then we have Judaism, Gnosticism, Confucianism—on and on. You get the idea. Each religion is a separate but equally legitimate path to the same God. The journeys may be different but the destination is the same.

Most religions do have several similar qualities. Fundamentally, most acknowledge the existence of a divine being, beings, or essence. Many religions agree that something—whether sin or a need for enlightenment or a lack of belief—has created a barrier between humans and the divine. Most religious philosophies agree that, whatever the cause, we can overcome that barrier in our search to know the divine. As such, the majority of religions place an emphasis on living a moral life devoted to the pursuit of the divine; for many, this is done in part to achieve a more pleasant afterlife. With so much commonality, the "different paths, same destination" philosophy certainly seems quite reasonable.

In stark contrast to such an inclusive and harmonious view stands religious exclusivism. Religious exclusivism declares that only one religion is right or true. Adherents of many religions, including Christianity, make exclusive claims about their beliefs and practices, including who God is and how we can relate to him. Christians declare persistently that theirs is the only right way to God, the only true religion. Understandably, this bothers and offends innumerable people, including many Christians themselves. Catholic theologian Rosemary Radford Ruether stated that "the idea that Christianity, or even the biblical faiths, could have a monopoly on religious truth is an outrageous and absurd religious chauvinism."[3] Plenty of people would agree with Rosemary; the idea that Christianity is the only way to God is not only exclusive but arrogant. No matter what a person believes, if he or she is sincere in that belief, who are you to say they're wrong?

Sincerity in Faith

Have you ever met someone who followed a different

Jesus opened the pathway for each of us to have a direct, personal relationship with God.

religion and been a bit embarrassed by—or even jealous of—their earnest devotion to their faith? Perhaps they seemed more committed to their beliefs than you sometimes feel about your own. Maybe they seemed to be making a more wholehearted effort to live out their faith than you in living out yours. Whatever the reason, you can *feel* their dedication, faithfulness, and piety. In the light of such sincerity, the exclusionary nature of saying that only one religion is right feels not only narrow-minded but downright disrespectful.

In Western culture especially, withholding perceived or actual judgment of others' choices is held in high esteem. Even if you wildly disagree with someone's lifestyle, it's more socially acceptable to hold your tongue and "let them live their life."

This approach has been reinforced by what is sometimes called "recovery theology," popularized by organizations like Alcoholics Anonymous (AA). It's hard to overstate the excellent work AA and organizations like it do to help millions of people break free from addiction. Members of AA follow a structured twelve-step program, which includes an admission that "since we could not restore ourselves to sanity, some Higher Power must necessarily do so."[4] Step 3 of AA's program states plainly that "the effectiveness of the whole A. A. program will rest upon how well and earnestly we have tried to come to a decision to turn our will and our lives over to the care of God *as we understood him.*"[5]

Members of AA are encouraged to identify and rely on their own definitions of a higher power. This could be anything from the God of a particular religion to the universe as a whole to AA itself. There should be no judgment or criticism of another person's chosen higher power—as long as it helps them recover. This seems both understandable and practical. What does it matter, really, as long as the desired outcome is met? If someone is sober and healing, who cares whether that person's definition of God matches your own?

So when Christians—or anyone, for that matter—come along and claim that *their* God is the only true higher power, that seems irrational and even destructive. Where's their tolerance? In the United States, many people point to the nation's history to demonstrate that religious tolerance is a cornerstone of the culture. After all, if the country was founded on the principle of freedom of religion, then how dare someone say that everyone has to agree with his or her particular religious beliefs? That's controlling, unfair, and intolerant. You can believe whatever you want—that's your prerogative— but don't tell *me* what to believe. That's not any of your business anyway. Everyone should be able to adhere to the religion or philosophy that best aligns with their

---

Christianity is not a rulebook, a set of rituals, or a code of laws; it is a relationship with God.

---

thoughts and worldviews.

Examining Christianity

These are all good, fair points. The concerns raised are valid and sensible. If you're a Christian, you may have heard some of these very same statements. If you're not a Christian, it's possible you've expressed the above sentiments yourself—frankly, that may be true for many Christians, too. It's important to know that it's OK to have these questions, doubts, and concerns. It's not comfortable or fun to tell someone they're wrong, and it's no picnic to be told you're wrong, either. So why is this perceived narrowness part of Christianity to begin with?

Let's spend some time examining what Christianity actually *is*. Often people argue not against true Christianity but a caricature of it. Maybe you grew up in church hearing "the gospel" every Sunday but you still don't quite understand what it means. Maybe you've never cracked open a Bible. Maybe you used to believe but have lost your faith. No matter where you're coming from, try to clear your mind of presuppositions and biases (whether for or against Christianity) and take a fresh look at what the Bible actually says about following Jesus.

The Gospel: Christianity's Central Claim

Christianity centers on the gospel of Jesus Christ. As we discussed back in chapter 2, "gospel" comes from the Greek word *euangelion,* which means simply "good news." So to put it another way, Christianity centers on the good news of Jesus Christ—his message to humankind. Maybe you've heard the term "the gospel" thrown around but you're not sure what it means. Let's dive in together.

To understand the good news, we first have to be sure we grasp the bad news. Before Adam and Eve disobeyed God, humans and God shared life together in the Garden of Eden. But as I've said, Christians believe that sin fractured our relationship with God and turned the world into something it wasn't meant to be. And as in any relationship, when we've hurt, betrayed, or violated the other party, we must make amends in order to restore that relationship. But the scary part is that there's nothing we could ever say or do to fix this problem. The gap between us and the divine is much too big. Sin and death infected our world, and there's nothing we can do that will restore it.

Feeling hopeless? Don't despair; it's time for the good news. Christians believe that God stepped in to repair our relationship. Knowing that we could never find our way back to him on our own, God came to us through Jesus. While here, Jesus lived a sinless life—though not because he was never tempted. He fully experienced human life, with all its frustrations, emotions, and temptations.[6] But because Jesus was also divine, he was able to withstand the impulse to give in to sinful temptations. He spent the last years of his life traveling and teaching others about who God is, the love God offers to each person, and how to live a righteous life. Many of the religious leaders at the time felt threatened and angered by Jesus's teachings, which they considered to be blasphemous. Ultimately, Jesus was arrested, tortured, crucified, and died, though he had done nothing wrong. Christians believe that in that moment, Jesus—who himself was sinless—shouldered the burden of all our sins and suffered the punishment each one of us deserves.

But the story didn't end there. Three days later, Jesus rose again, conquering sin and death in a way we never could. But still, the story isn't over. As a result of Jesus's sacrificial death and victorious resurrection, Jesus opened the pathway for each of us to have a direct, personal relationship with God. One helpful way to understand this crucial concept is to think of Jesus as the bridge between us and God—between humanity and the divine. Because of this bridge, we're able to receive forgiveness for our sins and ultimately eternal life with God. This is all summed up in the famous verse John 3:16: "For God so loved the world that he gave his one and only Son, that whoever believes in him shall not perish but have eternal life."

Much of the Jewish Law (found in the Hebrew Bible or what many Christians call the Old Testament) details various processes that must be followed and sacrifices that must be made in order to become right with God again after one has sinned. In the Christian understanding, Jesus came to earth as a fulfillment of these laws. Jesus's death acted as the ultimate sacrifice—the ultimate gesture of God's love—for all humankind, freeing us from the bonds of sin and sacrificial laws. Through his sacrifice, we can be saved.

Often in casual conversation, when we talk about needing to be "saved" from something, we're not speaking in religious terms at all. We want to be saved from financial debt, an illness, death, or even more casual things like a bad date or boring meeting. While Christians believe that faith impacts every aspect of life, removal from uncomfortable situations isn't the core meaning of salvation here. In this context, salvation refers to deliverance from eternal separation from God. And God offers that salvation freely to anyone and everyone.

This "good news" stands in contrast with the message of many other religions. In essence, most religions convey something like this: "In order to earn salvation, you need to do these things and live this way." For instance, Buddhists believe that to reach Nirvana, a person must follow the Noble Eightfold Path, a process of personal effort and discipline to end suffering. Hindus believe that one reaches Moksha—freedom from this world and the cycle of death and reincarnation—by practicing self-sacrifice, meditation, and certain levels of self-realization. Muslims believe that Allah grants Paradise to those who live a life of moral uprightness, using the Five Pillars as basic guidelines. In contrast, Christianity says, "What needed to happen for you to be saved has been done. You could never do enough or be good enough to earn it through your words or actions. Salvation is a gift from God, given to you through Jesus." At its core, the Christian gospel is a joyful message of divine love, salvation, and redemption.

Jesus as the Way

This is why you hear Christians talking of Jesus as "the way to God." We have each lost our way and need to find the path back to God. Christians believe God provided just that. Jesus made this clear in a conversation with his disciples: "I am the way and the truth and the life. No one comes to the Father except through me."[7] He didn't say he *knew* or *taught* the way, the truth, and the life; he said he *is* the way, the truth, and the life. Christianity is not a rulebook, a set of rituals, or a code of laws; it is a relationship with God. Jesus is the way to God precisely because he is the truth of God and the life of God.

The Apostles later taught the same. We're told

that one day Peter, one of the original twelve disciples, healed a crippled man, much to the amazement of onlookers. When the Jewish leaders saw the man and heard Peter speaking to the people, they demanded to know by what name or power Peter had healed him. Peter boldly answered, "It is by the name of Jesus Christ of Nazareth, whom you crucified but whom God raised from the dead, that this man stands before you healed.... Salvation is found in no one else, for there is no other name under heaven given to mankind by which we must be saved."[8]

From the Christian perspective, as reflected in Peter's words, we cannot save ourselves—nor can we choose our own way of salvation. The gospel calls us to this humble recognition. We must lay down any belief that we can figure out a way to God on our own. Biblical Christianity teaches that Jesus is the way to God; without him, there would be no way. It was Jesus's humanly impossible act of divine sacrifice that opened the way to God.

The Inclusivity of the Gospel

Here's what makes all this even more remarkable: Jesus came to earth for everyone—not just the wealthy, not just the well-educated, not just those who look or speak or act a certain way. Jesus died and rose for everyone. No one is excluded; no one is left out. He is the way for every human being in the world. The first time that followers of Jesus shared the gospel with others, people from a huge variety of ethnicities, languages, and backgrounds chose to believe in Jesus Christ.[9] The message of Jesus's death, resurrection, and love for humankind transcends all demographic barriers. The gospel is for everyone.

On one hand, it's true that Christianity could be labeled a "narrow" religion. Jesus himself said, "Enter through the narrow gate. For wide is the gate and broad is the road that leads to destruction, and many enter through it. But small is the gate and narrow the road that leads to life, and only a few find it."[10] That is, there is only one way to God, and that is through Jesus. But in this context, "narrow" doesn't mean "exclusive."

Christianity is not an American religion or a Western religion. It is not a white religion or an upper-class religion. Following Christ is for all people from all backgrounds in all places. As a matter of fact, Christianity is thriving in more regions around the world than any other religion, making it the world's most culturally diverse religion.[11] God created each of us with love, and Jesus came to save the entire human race, not one group or kind of people. We took a look at John 3:16 a bit earlier, but that portion of the Bible continues with a very insightful verse: "For God did not send his Son into the world to condemn the world, but to save the world through him."[12]

Jesus came so that whoever believes in him will not perish but will have eternal life. God sent his Son to save the world. Paul further illustrates this when he writes that living peaceful, godly, holy lives "is good, and pleases God our Savior, who wants all people to be saved and to come to a knowledge of the truth. For there is one God and one mediator between God and mankind, the man Christ Jesus, who gave himself as a ransom for all people."[13] Though it seems paradoxical, the "narrow way" is wide open to the entire world. The gospel is not a restrictive command but a simple invitation from Jesus to all who are interested.

The Consequences of Sin

That all sounds wonderful, but what's much harder to contend with is the idea that if you don't accept this invitation, you'll be sent to a place of eternal punishment—to hell. This implication of the "Jesus is the only way" concept is perhaps the most challenging aspect of Christianity. Though uncomfortable and awkward to talk about, hell is a part of theology that can't be ignored when trying to take an honest look at Christianity. As we discussed in the last chapter, according to Christian theology, humanity turned against God through sin. Sin occurs when our thoughts, attitudes, or actions are self-serving or self-indulgent to the detriment of others or our relationship with God.

Think about your own life. We know ourselves; we know the darkness in our hearts. This may be the part of Christianity with the most empirical evidence. Sadly, we verify the existence of sin every day—sometimes in terrible ways, sometimes in very ordinary ways. Most people try hard to live good lives, regardless of whether they believe in God. Yet our best efforts often fall far short of even our own expectations.

Recently, I was in the grocery store in a hurry to get out of there. I hunted for the shortest line and thought I had chosen wisely . . . until the family just before me got to the front. The woman pulled out a stack of coupons, which the cashier meticulously (a.k.a., *slowly*) scanned before slipping each one into a locked safe. I lost all patience, both with the family and the cashier. But then I heard the family talking. They were counting pennies, not quite making ends meet. Shame overcame me. I had judged that family, put my self-interest above patience and grace, and let myself get angry with a cashier just trying to do his job. I had messed up. I'm sure you've had similar experiences.

We hope God grades on a curve, because we're not perfect but we're pretty good. But there's an interesting way to frame this issue. Let's look at what Dr. Louis Markos writes:

> One of the reasons that hell is such a difficult concept is that so many of us (myself included) tend to think about heaven and hell by means of a false analogy. Life, we think, is like college. If we get an A in life, we go to heaven; if we get an F, we go to hell. To the modern mind, such a scenario seems unfair, a violation of our firmly held belief that all men are created equal. But what if there are two colleges: a college of heaven and a college of hell? . . . And what if God, out of love for us and our freedom, lets us choose which college we enroll in?[14]

In his book *The Problem of Pain,* theologian C. S. Lewis discusses Jesus's parable of the sheep and the goats. In this teaching, the sheep (representing compassionate people) go to heaven, while the goats (symbolizing those who showed no compassion to others) are banished to what Jesus calls "the eternal fire prepared for the devil and his angels."[15] Lewis points out that in this parable, "the saved go to a place prepared for *them,* while the damned go to a place never made for men at all."[16] There is a monumental implication in these words of Jesus: God didn't create man for hell nor hell for man. Human beings were not intended for hell, nor hell for human beings. But herein lies the problem. Dr. Markos continues:

> When we continually choose ourselves and our desires over the one who created us and what he wants for us, we *dehumanize* ourselves, separating ourselves from our creator and designed purpose. By a process that is as much theological as it is psychological, we surrender the part of ourselves that makes us human.
>
> Lewis illustrates this point most effectively in *The Great Divorce* . . . [in which] he takes his readers on a peculiar bus ride from hell to heaven, during which saved souls try to convince the damned *even now* to forsake their sins and embrace the love and mercy of God.
>
> At one point Lewis focuses on the damned soul of a garrulous, grumbling woman who won't cease her pity-party long enough to listen to the saint

sent to help her. To Lewis, she does not seem an "evil" woman, only a grumbler. But that, his guide tells him, is the whole point: Is she a "grumbler, or only a grumble"?[17]

That is, is she still a person or has she become only the essence of her sin? Has she dehumanized herself completely? If there's even an ember of humanity left inside of her, the love of God can nurse the flame till it blazes again, but if all that is left is ashes, nothing can be done.[18]

For justice to be done, wrongs have to be treated as what they are—wrong. But, we say, I'm no murderer; my wrongs aren't that . . . well, wrong. There's a difference in getting frustrated with a cashier and robbing the grocery store. Right? Well, yes and no. Not all sins are equally atrocious, nor do they bring equal consequences. Several biblical authors describe some sins as worse than others or deserving of a more severe response.[19] There are several aspects that may make one sin more serious than another, including intentionality, knowledge of God's commands, persistence, and the number of people impacted.[20]

But the Bible is also clear that all sins are equal in the sense that they isolate us from God, damaging our relationship.[21] In this way, all sin—regardless of its severity—is to be avoided. Jesus said:

> You have heard that it was said to the people long ago, "You shall not murder, and anyone who murders will be subject to judgment." But I tell you

that anyone who is angry with a brother or sister will be subject to judgment. Again, anyone who says to a brother or sister, "Raca" [an Aramaic term of contempt], is answerable to the court. And anyone who says, "You fool!" will be in danger of the fire of hell. Therefore, if you are offering your gift at the altar and there remember that your brother or sister has something against you, leave your gift there in front of the altar. First go and be

Truth is narrow, but God's grace is wide.

reconciled to them; then come and offer your gift.... You have heard that it was said, "You shall not commit adultery." But I tell you that anyone who looks at a woman lustfully has already committed adultery with her in his heart.[22]

Seem a little radical? That's because it is. While sins differ in their offensiveness, sin of any kind separates us from God and who we're meant to be. Jesus said and did a lot of unconventional things, including affirming that justice and love matter more than rituals and tradition. He completely shook religious, societal, and cultural norms. Christians believe he taught these fresh insights in an attempt to help us better understand God's character and message of hope.

The Exclusivity of Truth

Now let's circle back to that illustration of God sitting on top of a mountain, with many paths by which to reach him. Despite the picturesque quality of this theory, there are a few fundamental flaws. While there are some commonalities in virtually all religions, several religions have little in common. If two philosophies have completely different claims about the same topic, can both be right?

Take the cornerstone of religion—the concept of the divine. In other words, what's at the top of the mountain? For Hindus, there are many gods; for some Buddhists, there is no god at all. For Muslims, there is only one God; for Christians, there is one God in triune form: Father, Son, and Spirit. These four views—a small sampling of the religions and philosophies in the world—all say something significantly different. To say otherwise is an insult to the uniqueness of each religion and its views.

The most basic laws of logic teach that two contradictory statements cannot both be true. A and *not-A* cannot both be true in the same way at the same time. Employing this logic, all the claims made by these religions could be false, but only one could be true. In many ways, far from being paths on the same mountain trying to reach the same God, these religions aren't even on the same planet. They each have exclusive claims as to what truth is. It's simply not rational to see all religions as divergent but equally true paths to the same end; to do so is to ignore the reality of each religion's actual belief system.

It's important here to distinguish between preferences and truth. For instance, I like mint chocolate chip ice cream. You might prefer strawberry. There's no conflict there—other than the decision of which ice cream to buy. Ultimately, we're both eating ice cream; to say we're eating broccoli would be false. Truth is always intolerant of error. One plus one always equals two. You could call that intolerant or narrow, but it's the nature of truth. We like our doctors and our pilots to operate within a narrow truth; we want them to do surgery on the correct knee and land the plane on the right runway. We want those who create new medicines and vehicles and appliances to be appropriately intolerant of error. In so many areas of life, we rightly see intolerance, exclusivity, and narrowness as good and necessary qualities.

The Limits of Sincerity

But what happens when a Christian and a Muslim, for example, feel equally convinced that their religion is teaching the one correct truth? While sincerity of belief carries emotional power, sincerity simply has no logical connection with truth. Years ago, an American football player, Jim Marshall of the Minnesota Vikings, got the ball and ran with all his heart. He broke tackles all the way down the field and across the goal line for a touchdown. But he had run the wrong way. In his celebration, thinking he was right, he threw down the ball and ultimately scored for the other team. He was very sincere in his efforts, but he was sincerely wrong. The other team got the points.

No matter how wholeheartedly we embrace our beliefs, our sincerity cannot change reality; it never does. Believing something is true doesn't make it so, because truth is independent of our beliefs about it. Most of us can identify with thinking we're right about something only to realize later we were wrong. This happens to me all the time. I think I sent an e-mail, but when I check, I see it sitting in my draft folder because I forgot to hit send. I've thought I was driving in the right direction, but a quick GPS check reveals that I'm going the wrong way. It's embarrassing but fairly inconsequential.

You may be very sincere in your religious beliefs, but if they're wrong, you're in trouble; you're driving your life in the wrong direction. God is who he is, independent of our beliefs about him. Being wrong about God is serious. It matters—a lot. It is for this very reason that Christians are compelled to tell others about Jesus, whom they believe to be the only way to God and eternal life. In fact, this is why followers of many religions feel responsible for converting others to their faith.

Tolerance: Stopping Too Short

But where's their tolerance for other beliefs? you may be thinking. Of course everyone has the right to believe whatever they want to believe. You have a right to your own thoughts and beliefs, just as you have a right to your own deeds and actions. But that doesn't make your beliefs true or your actions good. Religious tolerance doesn't mean that we say everyone is right; rather, tolerance means coexisting peacefully alongside those with whom we disagree.

It may surprise you to learn that Christianity teaches that tolerance isn't enough. It's not enough merely to tolerate someone else's belief system, opinions, or existence. We should aim higher. Jesus says we are to love and do good to others—*all* others, even "our enemies." To Jesus's original audience, "enemies" would have signified strangers or outsiders, meaning those of a race or religion not your own (closer to our modern use of the phrase "those different from you"). While tolerance is a passive endeavor, love requires action.

As Penn Jillette, an American entertainer and advocate for atheism, has explained, "How much do you have to hate somebody to not proselytize? How much do you have to hate somebody to believe that everlasting life is possible and not tell them that?"[23] Christians believe we shouldn't settle for tolerance; we should reach out in love. Imagine you discovered the cure for cancer.

The cure you discovered works every time, on every person, regardless of the type, advancement, or location of the cancer. Now imagine someone refusing the treatment, saying, "Wait, that's too narrow. There are plenty of experimental treatments for cancer. Don't insist on just one." What sense would that make? From the Christian perspective, Jesus Christ is the cure that works every single time for every single person—the way to God for everyone. Truth is narrow, but God's grace is wide.

Of course, all this naturally raises a follow-up question: Is Jesus really God? It's understandable for Christians to endeavor to spread the message of what they believe to be the key to salvation, but how do they know what they're saying is true? How do they know Jesus is who he says he is?

Endnotes for Chapter 4

1. John Lennon and Yoko Ono, "Imagine," *Imagine,* Apple Records, 1971.

2. Christine Lee, "Irving Neighborhood Ranked America's Most Diverse," *NBC DFW,* January 1, 2013, http://www.nbcdfw.com/news/local/Irving-Neighborhood-Ranked-Americas-Most-Diverse-185375252.html.

3. Rosemary Radford Ruether, "Feminism and Jewish-Christian Dialogue," in *The Myth of Christian Uniqueness: Toward a Pluralistic Theology of Religions,* eds. *John H. Hick and Paul F. Knitter* (Eugene, OR: Wipf & Stock Publishers, 1987), 141.

4. *Twelve Steps and Twelve Traditions* (Alcoholics Anonymous World Services, 1953), 107.

5. Ibid., 34-35, emphasis their own.

6. *The Holy Bible,* Matthew 4:1-11.

7. *The Holy Bible,* John 14:6.

8. *The Holy Bible,* Acts 4:10, 12.

9. See *The Holy Bible,* Acts 2:1-41.

10. *The Holy Bible,* Matthew 7:13-14.

11. According to a PEW study, "Christians are also geographically widespread—so far-flung, in fact, that no single continent or region can indisputably claim to be the center of global Christianity." As of 2011, 26% of all Christians live in Europe, 37% in the Americas, 24% in sub-Saharan Africa, and 13% in Asia and the Pacific. See "Global Christianity – A *Report on the Size and Distribution of the World's Christian Population, "Pew Research Center,* December 19, 2011, http://www.pewforum.org/2011/12/19/global-christianity-exec/.

12. *The Holy Bible,* John 3:17.

13. *The Holy Bible,* 1 Timothy 2:3-6.

14. Louis Markos, PhD, "Would a Loving God Send Someone to Hell?" Explore God, https://www.exploregod.com/articles/would-a-loving-god-send-someone-to-hell.

15. *The Holy Bible,* Matthew 25:41.

16. C. S. Lewis, *The Problem of Pain* (San Francisco: HarperSanFrancisco, 2001), 127.

17. C. S. Lewis, *The Great Divorce* (San Francisco: HarperSanFrancisco, 2001), 77.

18. Markos.

19. See *The Holy Bible*, John 19:10-11, Matthew 7:3, Matthew 23:24.

20. *The Holy Bible*, Numbers 15:22-30; Luke 12:47-48

21. *The Holy Bible*, Romans 3:23, 5:16; James 2:10; 1 John 3:4.

22. *The Holy Bible*, Matthew 5:21-24, 27-28.

23. Penn Jillette, "Penn Says: A Gift of a Bible," *Crackle*, originally posted December 8, 2008.

CHAPTER FIVE

Is Jesus Really God?

"Jesus is just alright with me. Jesus is just alright, oh yeah."
—*"Jesus Is Just Alright," Arthur Reid Reynolds*[1]

I can barely type those lyrics without humming the melody in my head! I hope I didn't get it stuck in yours. But whether you're a music buff or have no idea what song I'm talking about, you might identify with the sentiment expressed above. Most people agree with Arthur in his song made famous by The Byrds and The Doobie Brothers. In fact, the majority of people *like* Jesus—what he stood for, how he lived his life, how he treated people. Almost no one sees him as a bad guy, regardless of their religious backgrounds (or lack thereof).

What's truly astonishing is that many major world religions also have a positive view of Jesus. Within Islam, Jesus is considered a prophet, a messenger of Allah, and a worker of miracles.[2] Muslims acknowledge the significance of Jesus within monotheistic religion and hold him in high regard. While Hinduism comprises a diverse set of beliefs over a variety of traditions, many Hindus embrace Jesus as a *sadhu,* a holy man. Some understand him to be the perfect embodiment of *dharma.*[3] Some Buddhists regard Jesus as a *bodhisattva* who dedicated his life to the welfare of all humans.[4] In fact, the fourteenth-century Zen master Gasan Jōseki indicated that the teachings of Jesus as recorded in the gospels were said by an enlightened man.[5] Even outside of these belief systems, Jesus is commonly considered to be a great example of how to live your life well. His teachings contain positive moral principles, and he led a life filled with love, compassion, and self-sacrifice.

But then you get to the Christians. Christians say yes, Jesus was a prophet, a miracle-worker, a holy man, and an enlightened man—but there's more to him than that. Jesus wasn't *just* a man; he was (and is) God incarnate.[6] That means that Christians believe Jesus was both fully human and fully God. As a man, Jesus underwent the full spectrum of human emotions and experiences, including joy, anger, pain, and temptation. He ate, slept, and wept. But as God, Jesus lived a life free of sin. Christians believe that Jesus defeated sin and death through his resurrection.

Because I'm a pastor, it's not uncommon for people to engage me in spiritual conversations. Recently an acquaintance emailed me to do just that. In our exchange, I asked him what he thought of Jesus. He responded, "Well, according to the Bible, he was a man of many talents and a very influential person in his time. Do I believe that he is the only Son of God? That answer is a resounding no." He's certainly not alone in that line of thinking. So why *do* Christians think Jesus was more than just a man? Is Jesus God? How can we answer those questions?

The Historical Jesus

Perhaps the best place to start is the simplest: Was Jesus even a real person? Some say that Jesus never existed; he's a legend, a myth, a nice story. All fiction, no fact. However, most trained historians reject that claim outright based on the evidence available. Though many presume that Jesus is mentioned only within the pages of the Bible, Jesus's existence is actually supported by multiple outside sources.

The Roman historian and senator Tacitus referred to Jesus, Jesus's execution by Pontius Pilate, and the existence of early Christians in Rome in his writings from 116 CE.[7] Pliny the Younger, the Roman governor of Bithynia in Asia Minor, wrote a letter to Emperor Trajan around 112 CE, asking for advice on how to handle legal proceedings against those accused of being Christians. At one point in his letter, Pliny writes that the Christians were "in the habit of meeting on a certain fixed day before it was light, when they sang in alternate verses a hymn to Christ, as to a god, and bound themselves by a solemn oath, not to any wicked deeds, but never to commit any fraud, theft or adultery, never to falsify their word, nor deny a trust when they should be called upon to deliver it up."[8]

The historical evidence overwhelmingly supports the reality of Jesus's life, his death on the cross, and the early devotees who eventually became known as Christians. As scholar Craig Blomberg puts it, "Biblical scholars and historians who have investigated the issue in detail are virtually unanimous today in rejecting this view [that Jesus never existed], regardless of their theological or ideological perspectives."[9]

What Was Jesus Called?

We can begin to gain insight into who Jesus was from the names and titles Jesus's contemporaries used to describe him. A few centuries before Jesus was born, the Hebrew Bible (known by Christians as the Old Testament) was translated into Greek. This famous Greek version is called the Septuagint, and people in Jesus's day were familiar with it. When reading Hebrew texts aloud, it was Jewish practice to substitute the word *Adonai*, which means "lord," for Yahweh, the name of God, because God's name was regarded as too sacred to be said. In the Septuagint, the Greek term *kyrios* is used to translate *Adonai*. For first-century Jews, applying the title *Adonai* to anyone other than God was unthinkable— it was blasphemy. And yet *kyrios* is used to refer to Jesus multiple times in the New Testament. Scholars struggle to explain how it was possible for Jewish people in the first century to suddenly call a carpenter from Nazareth "LORD," equating him with the one true God.

Similarly, the Greek word *theos*, which translates to "God," is usually reserved for God the Father. But despite this, seven passages explicitly refer to Jesus using the word *theos*.[10] Jesus was called the King of kings and Lord of lords,[11] our great God,[12] and our Lord and Savior.[13] Those who followed him believed Jesus was the fulfillment of Isaiah's prophecy, which spoke of a child who would "be called Wonderful Counselor, Mighty God, Everlasting Father, Prince of Peace."[14] Paul, who had once been a fervent persecutor of Christians, wrote of Jesus: "God exalted him to the highest place and gave him the name that is above every name, that at the name of Jesus every knee should bow, in heaven and on earth and under the earth, and every tongue acknowledge that Jesus Christ is Lord."[15] These are truly shocking words coming from a man trained in Jewish thought. The weight of these titles can't be easily dismissed.

What Did Jesus Say about Himself?

As we consider the possibility of Jesus's divinity, it's important to consider what Jesus claimed about himself. In short, did *Jesus* think he was God? If even he didn't buy it, then we can certainly dismiss the idea. One of the first ways we get to know anyone is by asking them questions and listening to what they say about themselves. Figuring out who Jesus is doesn't need to be all that different. The writers of the New Testament made it pretty easy to discover what Jesus had to say about himself—and he said a lot.

As recorded in the book of Luke, Jesus bookended his ministry with the assertion that he was the

Messiah about whom the Old Testament prophets had prophesied.[16] He stated several times that he was sent to earth by God, whom he called "Father."[17] He equated himself with God, declaring, "I and the Father are one."[18] Perhaps most shocking of all for his original Jewish audience, Jesus referred to himself by God's personal name, "I AM."[19] He used the "I am" phraseology not only to connect himself to God but also to make some other astounding self-identifications. Jesus said:

- "I am the bread of life."[20]
- "I am the light of the world."[21]
- "I am the gate for the sheep."[22]
- "I am the good shepherd."[23]
- "I am the true vine."[24]
- "I am the resurrection and the life."[25]

Jesus summarizes all this in a single verse: "I am the way, the truth, and the life."[26] Each "I am" statement echoes Old Testament images and events that prefigure the prophesied Messiah, all of which would have been recognized by Jesus's original audience. The message Jesus is trying to convey is clear: "Here I am! I'm the one you've been waiting for—the one the prophecies predicted!"

But if all that wasn't enough for us, we can also see Jesus's clear affirmation of his divinity in three specific scenes selected from many in the Bible. In this first one, Jesus is in Jerusalem, teaching and preaching about God's kingdom. Jewish religious leaders challenge him on many fronts, and the dispute gets heated.

At this [the Pharisees] exclaimed, "Now we know that you are demon-possessed! Abraham died and so did the prophets, yet you say that whoever obeys your word will never taste death. Are you greater than our father Abraham? He died, and so did the prophets. Who do you think you are?"

Jesus replied, "If I glorify myself, my glory means nothing. My Father, whom you claim as your God, is the one who glorifies me. Though you do not know him, I know him. If I said I did not, I would be a liar like you, but I do know him and obey his word. Your father Abraham rejoiced at the thought of seeing my day; he saw it and was glad."

"You are not yet fifty years old," they said to him, "and you have seen Abraham!"

"Very truly I tell you," Jesus answered, "before Abraham was born, I am!"

At this, they picked up stones to stone him, but Jesus hid himself, slipping away from the temple grounds.[27]

Does that seem like a pretty extreme reaction? Jesus's claims so enraged the Jewish leaders that their response to his words was to harm him physically. Why? Because they fully understood that Jesus was claiming outright to be God, the one and only I AM. It was uncomfortable; it was radical; it was unthinkable.

In our second scene, Jesus has just healed a paralyzed man on the Sabbath. When the Jewish leaders challenge him for doing "work" on a holy day of rest, Jesus says:

> "My Father is always at his work to this very day, and I too am working." For this reason they tried all the more to kill him; not only was he breaking the Sabbath, but he was even calling God his own Father, making himself equal with God.
>
> Jesus gave them this answer: "Very truly I tell you, the Son can do nothing by himself; he can do only what he sees his Father doing, because whatever the Father does the Son also does. For the Father loves the Son and shows him all he does. Yes, and he will show him even greater works than these, so that you will be amazed. For just as the Father raises the dead and gives them life, even so the Son gives life to whom he is pleased to give it.[28]

Yet again, the religious leaders want to kill Jesus. He's violating the Jewish Law by breaking the Sabbath. He's blaspheming by claiming to be equal with God and calling himself the Son of God. And then he says he has the ability to do whatever God the Father can do, including give life. Who *is* this guy? They're confused and outraged by what he says; he seems determined to violate and undermine their way of life.

In our final example, we find Jesus standing on trial before the Jewish high priest. We're told that the chief priests were looking for evidence to put Jesus to death and that many testified falsely against Jesus.

> Then the high priest stood up before them and asked Jesus, "Are you not going to answer? What is this testimony that these men are bringing

against you?" But Jesus remained silent and gave no answer.

Again the high priest asked him, "Are you the Messiah, the Son of the Blessed One?"

"I am," said Jesus. "And you will see the Son of Man sitting at the right hand of the Mighty One and coming on the clouds of heaven."

The high priest tore his clothes. "Why do we need any more witnesses?" he asked. "You have heard the blasphemy. What do you think?"

They all condemned him as worthy of death.[29]

There's no mistaking it. Jesus claimed to be God.

What Did Jesus Do?

But here's something even crazier: Jesus also *behaved* like he was God. He didn't just talk the talk. He walked the walk—even on water.[30] (What? Pastors can make jokes too, you know). This next story is a perfect example. When Jesus was in Capernaum, four men carried their paralyzed friend to see Jesus in the hope that Jesus would heal him. But when they got to the house where Jesus was preaching, the crowd was so large that the men couldn't get through to Jesus. Thinking creatively, they got on top of the house and dug a hole through the roof, lowering their friend down to Jesus. When Jesus saw their faith in him, Jesus looked at the paralyzed man and said, "Son, your sins are forgiven."[31]

Can you imagine what they must have thought?

You don't have to, because Mark records the thoughts of the religious leaders who heard Jesus: "Why does this fellow talk like that? He's blaspheming! Who can forgive sins but God alone?"[32] And that's exactly Jesus's point. The story continues:

> [Jesus] said to them, "Why are you thinking these things? Which is easier: to say to this paralyzed man, 'Your sins are forgiven,' or to say, 'Get up, take your mat and walk'? But I want you to know that the Son of Man has authority on earth to forgive sins." So he said to the man, "I tell you, get up, take your mat and go home." He got up, took his mat and walked out in full view of them all. This amazed everyone and they praised God, saying, "We have never seen anything like this!"

The Gospel of John records Jesus saying, "I will do whatever you ask in my name, so that the Father may be glorified in the Son. You may ask me for anything in my name, and I will do it."[33] Um, *what?* Jesus is saying we can pray *to him*? Prayer is reserved for God—just like worship. Yet multiple times in the gospels, we see people worshipping Jesus.[34] And he accepts it! Even though Jesus says in Luke 4:8, "Worship the Lord your God and serve him only."

How do you reconcile the two? How do you think *Jesus* reconciled the two? If Jesus believed that only God is worthy of our praise and yet he also accepted others' worship of him, Jesus must have believed that the two—God the Father and Jesus the Son—were one and the same.[35] And how remarkable that the people who also knew these teachings gave praise and worship to Jesus, a lowly carpenter, even after his death. Authors Robert M. Bowman Jr. and J. Ed Komoszewski put it this way:

> It was in this context of exclusive religious devotion to one God, the Lord, that the early Jewish followers of Jesus were expressing the same sort of devotion to Jesus. They worshipped him, sang hymns to him, prayed to him, and revered him in a way that believers in Judaism insisted was reserved for the Lord alone. To make matters worse, the Christians agreed that such honors were rightly given only to God—and then proceeded to give them to Jesus anyway![36]

That is, they continued to believe only God was worthy of such honor. But they also believed that Jesus was worthy . . . because Jesus and God were one and the same. (It's natural here to wonder if Christians believe in more than one God. Christians believe there is only one God, but he exists in three persons: Father, Son, and Holy Spirit. Together, they form the Trinity.[37] I promise we'll dig into the concept more in chapter 7.)

How could this be? What was so persuasive? What convinced them that Jesus was God? You guessed it. The resurrection.

Did the Resurrection Happen?

The entirety of Christianity hinges on the resurrection. Even the Bible says so: "If Christ has not been raised, our preaching is useless and so is your faith."[38] Pretty heavy stuff. Essentially, if the resurrection is a lie, so is the rest of Christianity. So? Did it happen? Was Jesus really resurrected? Well, quite simply, resurrection is humanly impossible. Death is final. Right? It's understandable to doubt or even outright reject the claim that Jesus died and then rose from the dead three days later. Jesus himself predicted his death and resurrection multiple times. But that doesn't get us too far in determining if that really happened.

Theologian William Lane Craig cites the following four historical facts as indicators of the truth of the resurrection story. He argues that while various theories can explain each of these facts individually, the only explanation that encompasses all four components is that Jesus was indeed resurrected from the dead.[39]

1. Jesus's burial
2. The empty tomb
3. The fact that multiple people, often in groups, claimed that Jesus appeared to them after his death
4. The origin of the followers' belief in his resurrection[40]

Let's walk through what happened all those years ago. Jesus died publicly, crucified by professional executioners. His body was placed in a tomb, which was sealed by a large stone, as was the custom of the time. Three days later, the tomb was empty. Almost no one disputes that. In fact, even the Roman guards meant to be watching the tomb corroborated this by claiming the disciples had stolen the body.[41] Then more than five hundred people claimed to see Jesus alive—not just isolated incidents but often in groups.[42] All anyone had to do to put those claims to rest and prove those people wrong was produce Jesus's body. But no one ever did.

Even a casual reading of the gospels reveals that the disciples didn't expect the resurrection to take place. After Jesus's death, they saw nothing in the cross but defeat. They were confused, scared, and sad. Even *they* didn't believe the news of the empty tomb at first; they had to be convinced. But convinced they were. For the rest of their lives, they maintained that Jesus had appeared to them in the flesh after his death, bearing the wounds of the crucifixion. And they didn't stop there. They said they didn't just see Jesus. They talked with him, touched his scars, walked with him, and ate with him. History tells us that soon after this, people began to die for their faith in Jesus—for their insistence in the truth of the resurrection.

One hypothesis that attempts to explain the empty tomb states that the resurrection was a hoax perpetrated by early Christians. This theory posits that followers of Jesus stole and hid his body in order to make it appear that Jesus was the Messiah and had risen from the dead. Thus the empty tomb. Craig's point here is that people don't willingly die for something they know is just a lie. These early Christian martyrs died because of their earnest belief in the truth of Jesus's resurrection—because of their personal experience with it. Even if you don't believe that Jesus rose, you can't deny that Jesus's followers were convinced that he did. They were certain enough that they were willing to face death rather than renounce their faith. That's hard to ignore.

Liar, Lunatic, Lord

Jesus assumed divine names and affirmed his equality with God; he claimed to heal the sick and to forgive sins. He accepted worship and said we could pray to him. No other major religious figure made the kind of claims about themselves that Jesus made of himself. Muhammad was clear that he was only a man; he directed people to Allah.[43] The Buddha never claimed to be salvation himself; he pointed people to the Noble Eightfold Path.[44] The Jewish prophets claimed only to be messengers of God, never God himself.

There's certainly nothing in either Jesus's words or actions to indicate that he was joking. That leaves us with three options: 1) Jesus was lying. He isn't God. 2) Jesus was delusional. He isn't God, but he thought he was. 3) Jesus was telling the truth. He is God. You may have heard this called the "liar, lunatic, or lord trilemma." Though he did not originate the argument, theologian C. S. Lewis's summation bears repeating. Here's how he put it:

> A man who was merely a man and said the sort
> of things Jesus said would not be a great moral
> teacher. He would rather be a lunatic—on the level
> with the man who says he is a poached egg—or else
> he would be the Devil of Hell. You must make your
> choice. Either this man was, and is, the Son of God:
> or else a madman or something worse.[45]

Though we of course can't prove Jesus's mental state, we do know that he uttered some of the most profound statements ever recorded—wisdom that has passed the test of time—so it seems unlikely that Jesus was a "madman." Was he a liar, then? Philosopher Peter Kreeft muses: "Why did thousands suffer torture and death for this lie if they knew it was a lie? What force sent Christians to the lions' den with hymns on their lips? What lie ever transformed the world like that?"[46] That is, if Jesus's followers knew the resurrection was a lie, would they be willing to endure persecution, ridicule, torture, and even death just to perpetuate a charade? They walked through life with Jesus, heard him teach and preach, and saw him die on the cross. In order to give their lives willingly to spreading the gospel of Jesus, they must have been truly convinced that a) Jesus was resurrected from the dead and therefore b) Jesus was the prophesied Messiah—the anointed one, their savior.

What Did His Followers Believe?

So what, exactly, did the first Christians believe? Thanks to the stories and letters recorded in the Bible, we can see the beliefs of some of Jesus's earliest followers. Let's take a quick look at three separate statements made by three different people, all written in the first century after Jesus's death. Each author makes a strong claim for Jesus being God within the first chapter of their books.

John: The Gospel Writer

John was one of the original twelve Apostles, and he was particularly close to Jesus—part of an inner core that included James and Peter.[47] John ate with Jesus,

---

Without money, without an army, without writing a word, a carpenter from Nazareth changed the course of history.

---

traveled with him, and worked alongside him. John opens his telling of Jesus's life with a description of Jesus (referred to as "the Word") that mirrors the opening of the book of Genesis: "In the beginning was the Word, and the Word was with God, and the Word was God. He was with God in the beginning. Through him all things were made; without him nothing was made that has been made. In him was life, and that life was the light of all mankind."[48]

Look back at that very first sentence. "And the Word was God." Bingo. John believed it—enough to write it down and share it with others so that they might learn who Jesus is. John is saying that Jesus has existed since the very beginning of time. He was there when the world was made, and indeed he gave life to humanity. Bold claims. I don't know about you, but that's not something I'd write about any of my friends.

Paul: The Converted Persecutor

Paul was a highly educated man, brought up as a Pharisee in "the strict manner of the law."[49] The Pharisees were an ancient Jewish group distinguished by their emphasis on the supreme importance of the Hebrew Law. Paul was especially zealous in his endeavor to adhere to the Pharisaical code. Such was his devotion to his training that in the earliest days of Christianity, Paul (also named Saul) actively tried to stamp out the movement. We're told that he approved of the execution of Stephen, the first Christian martyr, and attempted to destroy the nascent Christian church by entering homes and imprisoning those who believed in Jesus (they weren't even called Christians yet!).[50]

In fact, Paul was so antagonistic toward followers of what was then called "the Way" that he went to the high priest and, "breathing threats and murder against the disciples of the Lord," asked for permission to travel to the synagogue in Damascus in search of more believers to imprison back in Jerusalem.[51] But a funny thing happened on the way to Damascus. Paul heard the voice of Jesus speaking from heaven, and his life was forever changed.[52] As a result of his experience, he was baptized and began preaching the good news of Jesus in the very synagogue where he had hoped to eradicate the gospel.

Paul spent the rest of his years traveling to share the story of Jesus's life, death, and resurrection. He wrote several letters encouraging the burgeoning churches throughout the region. Let's take a look at a section of just one, a letter written to the church in the town of Colossae:

> The Son is the image of the invisible God, the firstborn over all creation. For in him all things were created: things in heaven and on earth, visible and invisible, whether thrones or powers or rulers or authorities; all things have been created through him and for him. He is before all things, and in him all things hold together. And he is the head of the body, the church; he is the beginning and the firstborn from among the dead, so that in everything he might have the supremacy. For God was pleased to have all his fullness dwell in him, and through him to reconcile to himself all things, whether things on earth or things in heaven, by making peace through his blood, shed on the cross.[53]

Sound familiar? Though written in Paul's own words, the sentiment echoes John's message. Paul says that Jesus is the image of God and reigns supreme in both creation and redemption; indeed, he has supremacy over "everything." Once again, we see bold claims—made especially so by Paul's background and education. It is through Jesus, says Paul, that God, humanity, and the earth will be reconciled. Clearly, Paul believed Jesus was more than just a man.

Unknown: The Author of the Book of Hebrews

Scholars debate the authorship of the book of Hebrews; as yet, there is no consensus. But while his or her identity is unclear, the author's perspective on Jesus is unmistakable—and it echoes Paul and John's. The author sums it all up in one sentence: "The Son is the radiance of God's glory and the exact representation of his being, sustaining all things by his powerful word."[54] Wow. Another statement reflecting the undeniable belief in Jesus's supernatural nature, a deep trust that Jesus is key to the creation and sustaining of this world.

Where the Head Meets the Heart

Up to this point, we've been looking at the chapter's question from the intellectual side. We've been using our heads to try to see if Jesus's divinity is possible, probable, or definite. But we would be remiss if we didn't take a moment to look at the heart—the testimonies of people's personal experiences with Jesus. We hit on this point somewhat back in chapter 2, but it's just as pertinent here.

We know that you can't prove a personal experience to be true or false—but does that really negate its value? We listen to how people's experiences inform their perspectives and beliefs on any number of things in life, from restaurant and product reviews to testimonials about a doctor's skill or a diet's effectiveness. We hear stories of lives changed for the better, and we applaud. There is power in sharing our experiences with others, because there is truth in them that applies not just to us but also to others—indeed even to all humanity. For Christians, their testimonies are exactly that: stories of changed minds, hearts, and lives with a central truth they feel compelled to share with others. There are innumerable beautiful stories of believers' personal experiences with Jesus Christ. Millions have felt Jesus's very real presence in their lives in myriad different ways: they heard a quiet voice or had a vivid dream or felt a convicting stirring of the heart.

Perhaps the idea of any of those things happening to you makes you uncomfortable. That's OK. Maybe that all sounds weird and you think those people have lost their grip on reality. That's fine, too. But it doesn't change much. No matter how we feel about someone else's experiences, the one thing we can't do is tell them that they did not have that experience.

Yes, faith comes in to play here. There's no way around it, and I don't want to hide from that fact. But through that faith, believers find certainty in their hearts that Jesus is real, relevant, and divine; they know because they've seen him at work in their lives. Something in them is not the same. I know because I've been there. Jesus has changed my life more times and in more ways than I could count. Though each person's relationship with Jesus is different, the beauty is that no matter a person's background, age, job, location, or financial situation, the Jesus they know is the same.

"Jesus Christ is the same yesterday and today and forever."[55]

When we broaden our scope, we can see the overwhelming, improbable influence the life of Jesus had on our world. It's hard to find a historical figure who has inspired more books, songs, and artwork than Jesus. Without money, without an army, without writing a word, a carpenter from Nazareth changed the course of history. As of 2015, nearly one-third of the world's population identified themselves as Christians—and that number is projected to continue to grow.[56] That means that 2.2 billion people around the world believe that Jesus is God. Medieval theologian Thomas Aquinas argued that if Jesus wasn't God incarnate, then an even more unbelievable miracle happened: "the conversion of the world by the biggest lie in history and the moral transformation of lives into unselfishness, detachment from worldly pleasures and radically new heights of holiness by a mere myth."[57]

Endnotes for Chapter 5

1. The Art Reynolds Singers, "Jesus Is Just Alright," by Arthur Reid Reynolds, recorded 1965, *Tellin' It Like It Is*, 1966. This song uses "alright" in the vein of 1960s slang to mean "cool" or "very good," as opposed to the current meaning of "OK." In 1969, The Byrds covered this song, and in 1973, The Doobie Brothers released their cover as a single. It reached #35, ultimately becoming the most popular version of the song.

2. Abdullah Yusuf Ali, *The Holy Qur-ān: English Translation & Commentary* (Kashmiri Bazar, Lahore: Sheikh Muhammad Ashraf, 1934).

3. Within Hinduism, dharma is the moral principle that governs duty, religion, and law. "For Hindus, dharma is the moral order of the universe and a code of living that embodies the fundamental principles of law, religion, and duty that governs all reality. The Hindu worldview asserts that by following one's dharma, a person can eventually achieve liberation from the cycle of death and rebirth (samsara)." "Dharma (Hinduism)," Berkley Center for Religion, Peace, and World Affairs at Georgetown University, https://berkleycenter.georgetown.edu/essays/dharma-hinduism.

4. Within Mahayana Buddhism, a bodhisattva is a being who, through compassion, refrains from entering nirvana in order to save others from suffering. That being is worshipped as a deity.

5. Senzaki, *101 Zen Stories* (Whitefish, MT: Kessinger Publishing, LLC, 2010), 34–35.

6. While Christians interpret the doctrine of the incarnation in different ways, all Christians believe in Jesus's divinity.

7. Cornelius Tacitus, *The Annals of Tacitus, Book XV*, chapter 44. See Alfred John Church, William Jackson Brodribb, and Sara Bryant, *Complete Works of Tacitus* (New York: Random House, Inc., reprinted 1942).

8. Pliny, *Letters*, transl. by William Melmoth, rev. by W.M.L. Hutchinson (Cambridge, MA: Harvard University Press, 1935), vol. II, X:96.

9. Craig L. Blomberg, "Jesus of Nazareth: How Historians Can Know Him and Why It Matters," in *Christian Apologetics: A Comprehensive Case for Biblical Faith* (Downers Grove, IL: IVP Academic, 2011).

10. Wayne Grudem, Bible Doctrine (Grand Rapids, MI: Zondervan, 1999), 236-237. See *The Holy Bible*, John 1:1, 18; John 20:28; Romans 9:5; Titus 2:13; Hebrews 1:8; 2 Peter 1:1.

11. See *The Holy Bible*, Revelation 17:14, 19:16.

12. See *The Holy Bible*, Titus 2:13.

13. See *The Holy Bible*, 2 Peter 1:11.

14. See *The Holy Bible*,, Isaiah 9:6.

15. See *The Holy Bible*, Philippians 2:9-11.

16. See *The Holy Bible*, Luke 4:16-21, in which Jesus reads Scripture from Isaiah before stating, "Today this scripture is fulfilled in your hearing." Ibid., Luke 24:27: "And beginning with Moses and all the Prophets,

[Jesus] explained to them what was said in all the Scriptures concerning himself."

17. See *The Holy Bible*, John 2:16; 3:16-18; 5:17; and 5:19-47.

18. *The Holy Bible*, New International Version © 2011, John 10:30.

19. *The Holy Bible*, Exodus 3:14.

20. *The Holy Bible*, John 6:35.

21. *The Holy Bible*, John 8:12.

22. *The Holy Bible*, John 10:7.

23. *The Holy Bible*, John 10:11.

24. *The Holy Bible*, John 15:1.

25. *The Holy Bible*, John 11:25.

26. *The Holy Bible*, John 14:6.

27. *The Holy Bible*, John 8:52-59.

28. *The Holy Bible*, John 5:17-21.

29. *The Holy Bible*, Mark 14:62-64.

30. See *The Holy Bible*, Matthew 14:22-33.

31. See *The Holy Bible*,, Mark 2:5.

32. See *The Holy Bible*, Mark 2:6-7.

33. See *The Holy Bible*, John 14:13-14.

34. See *The Holy Bible*,Matthew 2:2, 11; 14:33; 28:9, 17; Luke 24:52; John 9:38. Many scholars also consider bowing or kneeling to be a form of worship. See Matthew 8:2, 9:18, 15:25, 20:20; Mark 5:6.

35. See *The Holy Bible*,2 Samuel 22:4, 1 Chronicles 16:25, Psalm 18:3, Psalm 48:1, Psalm 96:4, Psalm 145: 3.

36. Robert M. Bowman Jr. and J. Ed Komoszewski, *Putting Jesus in His Place: The Case for the Deity of Christ* (Grand Rapids, MI: Kregel Publications, 2007), 30.

37. For more information about the doctrine of the Trinity, check out Norton Herbst, PhD, "What Is the Trinity?" Explore God, https://www.exploregod.com/articles/what-is-the-trinity.

38. *The Holy Bible*, 1 Corinthians 15:14.

39. William Lane Craig, *On Guard* (Colorado Springs, CO: David C. Cook, 2010), 219-220.

40. William Lane Craig vs. Bart D. Ehrman, "Is There Historical Evidence for the Resurrection of Jesus? The Craig-Ehrman Debate," (Worcester, MA: College of the Holy Cross, March 2006). An online transcript of this debate can be found here: https://www.reasonablefaith.org/media/debates/is-there-historical-evidence-for-the-resurrection-of-jesus-the-craig-ehrman/.

41. See *The Holy Bible*, Matthew 28:11-14. See also Ante-Nicene Fathers, Volume 1, ed. Alexander Roberts, James Donaldson, and A. Cleveland Coxe (Buffalo, NY: Christian Literature Publishing Co., 1885.)

42. See The Holy Bible, 1 Corinthians 15:3-8.

43. *The Qur'an*, Surah 18:110.

44. Walpola Rahula, *What the Buddha Taught* (New York: Grove Press, 1974), 1.

45. *Mere Christianity: a Revised and Amplified Edition* (New York: Harper

Collins, 2001), 52.

46. Peter Kreeft and Ronald K. Tacelli, *Pocket Handbook of Christian Apologetics* (Downers Grove, IL: InterVarsity Press, 2003), 63.

47. Many people believe John was the disciple reclining next to Jesus at the Last Supper. See *The Holy Bible*, John 13:23.

48. *The Holy Bible*, John 1:1-4.

49. *The Holy Bible*, Acts 22:3.

50. *The Holy Bible*, Acts 8:1.

51. *The Holy Bible*, Acts 9:1.

52. See *The Holy Bible*, Acts 9:3-19.

53. *The Holy Bible*, Colossians 1:15-20.

54. *The Holy Bible*, Hebrews 1:3.

55. *The Holy Bible*, Hebrews 13:8.

56. Pew Research Center, "The Changing Global Religious Landscape," April 5, 2017, http://www.pewforum.org/2017/04/05/the-changing-global-religious-landscape/.

57. Kreeft and Tacelli, 157.

CHAPTER SIX

Is the Bible Reliable?

"The existence of the Bible, as a book for the people,
is the greatest benefit which the human race has ever experienced.
Every attempt to belittle it . . . is a crime against humanity."
—Immanuel Kant[1]

"[The Bible] is full of interest. It has noble poetry in it;
and some clever fables; and some blood-drenched history;
and some good morals; and a wealth of obscenity;
and upwards of a thousand lies."
—Mark Twain[2]

This is a big one. Every chapter up until now has touched on the topic of the Bible, so it's time we took a look at its reliability, don't you think? The Bible has quite a few more critics than Jesus has. You very well may be one of them. It can be hard to know what to do with a book that people say is holy yet contains stories like: "[Elisha] turned around, looked at them and called down a curse on them in the name of the Lord. Then two bears came out of the woods and mauled forty-two of the boys."[3] Admittedly not my first choice for a Sunday sermon. Along with Twain, as quoted above, many condemn the Bible as racist, misogynist, violent, close-minded, irrelevant, inconsistent, contradictory, outdated, and untrustworthy.

And yet here we are. The Bible has carried tremendous influence around the world. Billions of people turn to it for comfort, guidance, and correction. It's largely respected as a work of great literature, but its reliability as a source of truth and its claim to be the divine word of God are under constant scrutiny—as they should be. Truth is important. It's perhaps harder than ever to know when we're getting straight facts. Anyone can write anything and post it online, with little to no accountability. The "news" shared on social media is often outdated, out of context, or simply not true. So how can we know what *is* true? How can we determine if the Bible is a reliable source of truth? Can we believe what its pages say about history, life, faith, and God? Can the Bible stand up to the tests of historians, archaeologists, and common sense?

An Introduction to the Bible

By no means is the Bible an easy read. I'd be lying to you if I said it was. The Bible is an elaborate, multigenerational, multicultural literary and historical feat. Scholars devote their entire lives to studying its pages, and even they disagree about some of their findings and interpretations. So yeah. The Bible can be intimidating. Let's start with some basic facts to help remove a bit of the mystery.

Though you often hear people refer to the Bible as a book, it's actually a collection of sixty-six books written by dozens of authors over hundreds of years.[4] Beginning with the creation of the world, the story told in the Bible spans millennia. It follows the history of the Israelites, details the life and ministry of Jesus, and concludes with a prophecy of the end of time. The content can be divided into several genres:

- Narrative: stories about historical people and events
- Poetry: lyrics, songs, and prayers that express emotions and ideas using distinctive language, literary styles, and rhythm
- Prophecy: messages conveying divine blessing or judgment on people and calling for a response from them
- Epistles: letters written by one or more people to churches and individuals, often addressing specific issues
- Wisdom literature: proverbs and sayings about living life well and making wise choices
- Legal codes: laws for ordering a just society
- Parables: imaginative stories that relate to life and illustrate a point
- Apocalyptic literature: writings that have to do with the end of the world[5]

The first five books (Genesis, Exodus, Leviticus, Numbers, and Deuteronomy) are known as the Torah (often translated as "Teaching" or "Law") or the Pentateuch (meaning "five scrolls"). These five books cover the creation of the world, the establishment of the nation and laws of Israel, and the Israelites' escape from slavery in Egypt. Following them are historical books, which recount the history of the Israelites after arriving in the Promised Land. After that, we find poetry and wisdom literature in the books of Job, Psalms, Proverbs, Ecclesiastes (which we looked at in chapter 1), and Song of Songs. Rounding out the Old Testament are the books of the prophets and the book of Lamentations, a series of poetic laments over the destruction of Jerusalem written by the prophet Jeremiah. The Old Testament spans roughly 2000–400 BC.

The New Testament picks up with the birth of Jesus about four hundred years later, starting with the four gospels, which are essentially biographies of Jesus's life. The Acts of the Apostles follows, and that book details the beginnings of the Christian Church. Twenty-one letters to various churches and individuals come next. They focus on Jesus's teachings, how to live a Christian life, and the lives of the people in the churches. The Christian Bible then concludes with the book of Revelation, perhaps the most controversial and confusing book of all, which uses imagery and symbolism to describe how God's redemptive plan for creation will come to fruition.

This is the biblical canon, the list of books officially

accepted and recognized as the product of divine revelation. The consensus is that the current canon was unofficially in place and being used by early churches by around 150 CE. In 367, Athanasius, the Bishop of Alexandria, published a universal list of the twenty-seven canonized books of the New Testament. Christians believe the books of the Bible were written by human authors with the divine guidance of God. As theologian J. I. Packer says,

> The Church no more gave us the New Testament canon than Sir Isaac Newton gave us the force of gravity. God gave us gravity, by his work of creation, and similarly he gave us the New Testament canon, by inspiring the individual books that make it up. Newton did not create gravity but recognized it.[6]

But there are certainly challenges to reading the Bible today. Some of it was composed over three thousand years ago. As a result, there are stories and figures of speech that just don't connect with or make sense to the average modern reader. There are references that assume cultural and historical knowledge that most of us don't have. Beyond that, relatively few people are reading the Bible in its original languages: ancient Hebrew, Aramaic, and Greek. So how can we know if the Bible we read today is reliable? Can it be counted on as a source of truth and guidance?

Validating the Bible

It's fair to say that no book has had more reach or impact on the world than the Bible. The full Bible has been translated into 698 languages, the New Testament into 1,548 languages, and at least one book of the Bible into 3,384 languages.[7] No other book is available in anywhere near that number of languages. Though it's difficult to obtain exact figures, almost everyone agrees that the Bible is the best-selling and most widely distributed book of all time. The words contained within its pages have influenced history, culture, politics, law, literature, music, and art. It's no overstatement to say that the world as we know it wouldn't exist without the Bible. As Leland Ryken wrote, "Everywhere we turn in the cultural past, we find the Bible. We cannot avoid it if we tried, and we will not understand our past without a knowledge of the Bible."[8]

But while the Bible's influence is impressive and undeniable, it doesn't do much when it comes to proving its credibility. To consider the reliability of the Bible, we can use the same measures of validation that we would for any other ancient book.

History in Archaeology

One way to validate the Bible's content is through archaeology. Did the people and places depicted in the Bible exist? Did the events described actually happen? Can we corroborate the stories told with outside evidence? Archaeologists have been digging in Egypt, Syria, Palestine, and Mesopotamia for hundreds of years—and only a fraction of the sites mentioned in the Bible have been excavated. New archaeological discoveries continue to expand our knowledge of the ancient world, from the names of cities and rulers to the type of pottery and weapons used in a certain place and time. Many of these archaeological finds have confirmed biblical accounts in terms of historical detail.

Take, for example, the Egyptian inscription called the Merneptah Stele or Israel Stele. It's the earliest textual reference to the nation of Israel outside of the Bible. It describes the pharaoh Merneptah's military victories, including a mention of an Egyptian military campaign in Canaan around 1210 BCE. It reads, "Israel is laid waste; its seed is not." Though the reference is short, study of the text and its implications has shown that it aligns with the biblical picture we have of Israel from this time.[9] Beyond this example, archaeologists have recovered the tomb of Uzziah, the king of Judah, whose death is recorded in 2 Chronicles 26:23. They have excavated much ivory in eighth-century-BCE Samaria, which fits the biblical description of King Ahab's palace as being "adorned with ivory."[10] The list goes on.

There are, of course, limits to what archaeology can tell us. While it can confirm that camels were domesticated during the time of Abraham[11] as Genesis indicates,[12] archaeology cannot affirm that God appeared to Abram, established a covenant with him, and changed his name to Abraham.[13] We can confirm that the villages of ancient Galilee had synagogues during the time of Jesus, but archaeology can neither prove nor disprove that Jesus preached a particular sermon on a particular day. But even with this limitation in mind, so many discoveries from ancient Egyptian, Hittite, Canaanite, Assyrian, and Babylonian cultures parallel biblical accounts that one prominent Jewish archaeologist stated, "No archaeological discovery has ever controverted a biblical reference. Scores of archaeological findings have been made which confirm in clear outline or exact detail historical statements made in the Bible."[14]

History in Literature

Outside of archaeology, ancient literary works can also corroborate biblical accounts. Historians depend greatly on ancient reports in order to reconstruct history. In fact, one of the most effective ways to determine a text's historical reliability is to compare it with information available to us from other contemporary sources. Of course, this is easier said than done for some time periods. Far more information about the United States in 1980 CE is available far more readily than information about Assyria in 980 BCE. Nevertheless, we do have written accounts that substantiate biblical texts.

Assyrian records attest to several kings, battles, and places mentioned throughout the Old Testament, and their timelines align. In his *Antiquities of the Jews,* the Jewish historian Josephus writes about Jesus's life, teaching, and death under Pilate's governorship. As we mentioned in the previous chapter, in 116 CE, the Roman historian Tacitus wrote of Jesus's execution and the early Christian movement. Pliny the Younger's writings regarding the meetings of early Christians, which we also examined in the last chapter, largely fit the description of the fellowship of believers given in Acts 2:42-47. Between 155 and 157 CE, Christian apologist Justin Martyr wrote a letter to Roman Emperor Antoninus Pius, asking him to spare Christians from persecution. In his letter, Justin Martyr defends the philosophy of Christianity, offers a detailed explanation of Christian practices, and suggests that the emperor verify the fact of Jesus's death by referring to official Roman records—specifically, the *Acts of Pontius Pilate.*[15] Beyond these examples, scholars also point to the fact that biblical names and writing styles are consistent with their cited time periods.

Objections to the Bible's Reliability

But even with mounting evidence, many valid questions remain about the Bible's reliability, particularly in regard to our modern versions. Let's take a look at the most common objections, which you may share.

Objection: Even if God inspired the original words, we don't have the original words.[16]

This is certainly true. We don't have the original pages of the books of the Bible. What we have are copies. But this issue isn't unique to the Bible; we face the same problem with nearly *all* ancient works. The clay tablets, papyrus, and parchment simply didn't last through the millennia. Then how can we know if what we're reading is an accurate representation of the original text? Scholars generally establish the credibility of ancient documents based on: 1) the nature and number of copies we have and 2) the number of years between the earliest copies and the original works. That is, how many years removed from the original is the copy in question? In this, the Bible is unparalleled.

What are some of the most well-known ancient texts you can think of? Plato's dialogues? Aristotle's teachings? The annals of the great Roman historians? For almost every ancient document you can name, a span of 700-1,450 years stretches between the original works and the earliest copy discovered thus far. When it comes to the Old Testament, the Dead Sea Scrolls are less than five hundred years removed from their original texts. We have two manuscripts containing almost the entire New Testament; they've been dated to just three hundred years from their originals. One fragment from the Gospel of John dates to a mere forty years of separation.[17]

And we have thousands of copies of biblical books. In fact, we have more early manuscripts of the New Testament than any other ancient text. According to Daniel Wallace, the executive director of the Center for Study of New Testament Manuscripts, we currently have over 5,800 Greek manuscripts that contain some portion of the New Testament. There are also thousands of early translations in languages such as Latin, Coptic, Syriac, Armenian, and others. When factoring these in, we wind up with more than 24,000 New Testament manuscripts. The closest work is Homer's *Iliad*, with around 1,800 manuscripts—the earliest dated at four hundred years removed from the original time of writing.[18] There's simply no comparison. Scholars Bart D. Ehrman and Bruce M. Metzger put it this way:

> In contrast with these figures [of other ancient works], the textual critic of the New Testament is embarrassed by a wealth of material. Furthermore, the work of many ancient authors has been preserved only in manuscripts that date from the Middle Ages (sometimes the late Middle Ages), far removed from the time at which they lived and wrote. On the contrary, the time between the composition of the books of the New Testament and the earliest extant copies is relatively brief. Instead of a lapse of a millennium or more, as is the case of not a few classical authors, several papyrus manuscripts of portions of the New Testament are extant that were copied within a century or so after the composition of the original documents.[19]

And we continue to discover new manuscripts and digitize old ones. We have more today than ever before, and every discovery helps to ensure the accuracy of our contemporary Bible. Every ancient manuscript is a chance to compare, analyze, and verify today's biblical text, an opportunity to uncover and examine any apparent inconsistencies.

Objection: The Bible is full of contradictions and inconsistencies.

Speaking of inconsistencies, doesn't the Bible contradict itself? It doesn't take long to discover what seem to be outright contradictions in the Bible. In fact, you encounter this on page one: Genesis chapters 1 and 2 contain two different creation accounts. In Genesis 1, God creates plants and animals, then human beings.[20] Genesis 2:5 says that "no shrub had yet appeared on the earth and no plant had yet sprung up" when God created humans.[21] Both of those things can't be true. We're only two chapters in, and already it seems like the author can't get the story straight! That's just one example; more could be listed. They all raise the question: If the Bible is filled with contradictions, how can it be a book of truth?

Once again, scholarship helps us make sense of it all. When you apply an understanding of ancient languages and literature and frame the text at hand in the cultural context of the time, most of these "discrepancies" turn out not to be contradictions at all. This is the case in Genesis. The book of Genesis employs an ancient artistic literary design known as telescoping. Genesis 1 tells the full story chronologically, while Genesis 2 "zooms in" on the creation of humankind. The second chapter overlaps the end of the first. That is, Genesis 2 is a telescoping of Genesis 1. Genesis 1 retells the story of creation in detail, ending with the creation of human beings. Chapter 2 picks up with the creation of humankind and tells that part of the story in more detail. These two chapters are complementary accounts, showing the artistry of the author.

Moreover, this is a great example of the importance of referring to the original language for added context. An understanding of the Hebrew words used for "plant," "shrub," and "vegetation" adds clarity here. By looking at the original meanings of the word and fitting Genesis 2:5 in the broader context of the book, we discover that the writer is actually referring to different types of plants. Professor Kenneth Mathews expounds:

> Genesis 2:5-7 is best understood in light of 3:8-24, which describes the consequences of sin. This is shown by the language of 2:5-6, which anticipates what happens to the land because of Adam's sin (3:18, 23). When viewed in this way, we find that the "shrub" and "plant" of 2:5 are not the same as the vegetation of 1:11-12. "Plant (*'ēśeb*) of the field" describes the diet of man which he eats only after the sweat of his labor (3:18-19) after his garden sin, whereas "seed-bearing plants" (*'ēśeb mazrîa' zera'*), as they are found in the creation narrative, were provided by God for human and animal consumption (1:11-12, 29-30; 9:3). These plants reproduce themselves by seed alone, but "plant," spoken of in 2:5, requires human cultivation to produce the grains necessary for edible food; it is by such cultivation that fallen man will eat his "food" (3:19).[22]

Other examples that have been raised are the seeming discrepancies between the accounts of Jesus's life. The gospel writers Matthew and Luke recount many of the same parts of Jesus's life, but sometimes their orders of events differ from each other. That makes it seem like the two gospels contradict one another, but the fact is, chronological accuracy is a modern concern, not an ancient one. Once you learn that ancient biographers (which is what Matthew and Luke were) often organized their content thematically, you can see that the differences in the texts simply reveal the purposes and themes important to each writer. In fact, the gospels fare well by modern standards of ancient biographies. They were written within a generation or two of the subject's life, and study has demonstrated that both Matthew and Luke made careful use of their sources.[23]

Think about this: If you were a police investigator with two separate eyewitness accounts that matched word for word, wouldn't you be suspicious? In all likelihood, the two witnesses have colluded. You would expect similar reports with minor differences. Imagine one person says she saw a dog and the other says he saw a cat. Contradictory? Not necessarily. Perhaps both a dog and a cat were at the scene. Theologian John Frame summarizes, "Evangelical writers have often said that although there are many Bible difficulties, nobody has ever *proved* the existence of a single error. This is true. It takes only a *possible* solution to a problem to refute the dogmatic assertion that there is *no* solution."[24]

Objection: Can't the message get lost in translation?

Remember the game Telephone? Did you play that as a kid? One person whispers a phrase to someone else, then that person whispers it to the next person. By the time it makes its way around the group back to the first person, the message is drastically different from the original saying. Now imagine if everyone playing was speaking a different language! When it comes to the Bible, not only are we working off copies, but those copies are translated from one language into another. Surely we've marred the original message; what we read today isn't the same as what was written all those years ago. How could it be?

Thankfully, modern Bible translation doesn't work like the Telephone game. Let's take a look at how translations of the Bible are created. We've mentioned that the Hebrew Bible was translated into Greek even before Jesus was born; that version was called the Septuagint.[25] As the books of the Bible were officially canonized into Scripture, more translations were made so that the gospel could be spread to more people in more areas of the world.

This included a fourth-century translation into Latin, known as the Vulgate. One thousand years later, a man named John Wycliffe completed the first full translation of the Bible into English, using the Vulgate as his primary source. In the seventeenth century, the king of England authorized forty-seven scholars to complete a new English translation, using the Greek, Hebrew, and Aramaic texts, with the Vulgate serving as a secondary resource. You may know this iteration as the King James Version. Since then, a variety of translations, in which scholars take a variety of approaches to the translation process, have been produced. These approaches fall somewhere on a scale from formal equivalence (word-for-word translations) to functional equivalence (meaning-for-meaning or thought-for-thought translations).[26]

Producing a translation of the Bible is no light undertaking. The process is time-consuming and tedious. To create a contemporary Bible translation, scholars, linguists, Bible experts, and other team members work together for years. Every word is checked and rechecked against ancient manuscripts in their original language, various commentaries, and past translations. The responsibility weighs heavily on those involved, and the painstaking process of creating a full Bible translation can take decades![27] Thanks to archaeology and technology, more resources are available to these scholars in more convenient ways than ever before. With every new discovery, our translations get even more accurate, and we get a chance to confirm what we have previously translated.

The Dead Sea Scrolls are a great example. Written and copied between the last three centuries BCE and the first century CE, these scrolls lay quietly in the Qumran Caves until sometime between late 1946 and early 1947, when local shepherds discovered them tucked away in jars, where they had been hidden.[28] Understandably, once they learned what these scrolls might be, scholars were eager to authenticate them. Experts confirmed the documents' antiquity through archaeology, paleography (the study of ancient writings), orthography (the study of letters and spelling), and carbon dating.[29] All methods arrived at the same conclusion: these are the oldest known Hebrew manuscripts of the Bible. Up until the discovery of these scrolls, the oldest Hebrew manuscripts of the Bible were Masoretic texts from around the tenth century CE. That means the Dead Sea Scrolls were written a *full millennium earlier*, making them an unprecedented resource when it comes to cross-checking the reliability of our modern biblical texts.

From within the Qumran Caves, excavators uncovered fragments from every Old Testament book except the book of Esther. Among the discoveries was what has become known as the Isaiah Scroll—a twenty-four-foot-long, well-preserved scroll containing the entire book of Isaiah. The Isaiah Scroll and another copy of Isaiah found in the caves proved to be of particular importance when it comes to determining biblical accuracy. Biblical scholar and theologian Gleason Archer writes:

> Even though the two copies of Isaiah discovered in Qumran Cave 1 near the Dead Sea in 1947 were a thousand years earlier than the oldest dated manuscript previously known (A.D. 980), they proved to be word for word identical with our standard Hebrew Bible in more than 95 percent of the text. . . . The five percent of variation consisted chiefly of obvious slips of the pen and variations in spelling.[30]

You read it right: 95 percent identical after one thousand years! Until this point, we knew that the ancient scribes had worked diligently and carefully to preserve their holy texts. But critics had always said that if we ever found earlier manuscripts of the biblical texts, they would reveal how far our modern versions have strayed from the originals. The Isaiah Scroll demonstrates just the opposite: it shows how accurate Scripture stayed over centuries.

Objection: There are so many interpretations. We can't know which is right.

OK, so say we do have reliable translations of the words that make up the Bible. That doesn't guarantee an accurate interpretation of what the words *mean*. We've all heard stories of people who did or said something outlandish or heinous "because the Bible told them to." It's commonplace to say "everyone has their own interpretation," as if there is no way to know which interpretation is correct.

While it may be true that God's thoughts and ways are not our thoughts and ways, it's also true that human language is generally adequate enough to convey meaning.[31] This isn't to say that the Bible is always easy to understand. There are several challenging, confusing passages in the Bible. As with any ancient work of literature, it's important to frame the books of the Bible within their original time periods, keeping in mind their original audience, their literary genre, and their historical context.

Misunderstandings of ancient conventions and

literary devices can lead people to distort the Bible. The writers of the Bible make skillful use of symbolism, metaphor, imagery, allegory, hyperbole, paradox, allusion, wordplay, and so much more. As in all poetry, not every word is meant to be read literally. In the past, people have twisted biblical passages to support their own agendas. Sadly, this will continue to happen. It's human nature to seek justification for our beliefs, actions, and prejudices; the distortion, misinterpretation, and misuse of the Bible does just that. There are countless examples of this, from perpetrators of genocide to cult leaders to hate groups. So how can we know when someone is misinterpreting a biblical text?

Because the Bible is the most studied book in the world, there is significant, high-quality scholarship on almost every passage. Scholars from multiple disciplines are trained in the original languages and are familiar with ancient history and relevant cultures. Generally speaking, trained scholars agree on the main point of most texts, while there sometimes remains significant disagreement on details and nuances. There are broadly well-accepted validations of any given text's meaning, such as the historical context, the meaning of each word, the grammatical structure of a sentence, and the characteristics of the literary genre.

Beyond this, one must consider any interpretation of a passage or section of the Bible in light of the Bible as a whole. How does the entire story hold together? Does that interpretation harmonize with the full message of the Bible—or does it clash? Early church leaders endeavored to make precise statements about crucial points of the Christian faith, expressing the meaning of the overarching story of the Bible. As early as the second century CE, we can see writers such as Ignatius and Irenaeus providing what came to be called "the rule of faith," which identified unity on fundamental approaches to interpretation of Scripture.[32] When trying to determine whether a specific interpretation can be considered valid, it can be helpful to refer back to these foundational agreements.

As our knowledge of the ancient world grows with greater access to more digitized sources from biblical times, scholars are gaining an ever-clearer picture of the context in which these texts were written. That increased knowledge leads to greater agreement on the meaning of each text. Unfortunately, this doesn't prevent people—both well-intentioned and malevolent—from posting or saying anything they'd like, whether or not their interpretation has any basis in scholarship.

Is the Bible God's Word?

We can see by looking at history, archaeology, and ancient manuscripts that the Bible proves reliable time and again. But I would be doing you a disservice if I stopped there. The fact is that Christians don't view the Bible as simply reliable; they consider it sacred. Just as Jesus claimed to be the Son of God, so is Scripture filled with claims that it is the Word of God. Every major Christian denomination affirms a commitment to the authority of Scripture as the source of God's truth.

Jesus did so as well. Though he received no formal religious training, Jesus knew and understood Scripture so deeply that the Jewish leaders of his day marveled at his knowledge and asked, "How did this man get such learning without having been taught?"[33] Indeed, Scripture was the basis for his own teachings; he believed in Scripture and often referred back to it. He quoted prophets by name and told his listeners that he was the fulfillment of those prophecies. During his time in the wilderness, Jesus resisted, refuted, and rejected Satan on three occasions with the words "It is written," before quoting Scripture as a source of power and truth.[34] There is no doubt that Jesus viewed Scripture as true, powerful, authoritative, and integral to one's faith and relationship with God.

Inspired by God

You may have heard claims that the Bible is "inspired." In this context, the concept applies to the relationship between God and those who wrote the pages of the Bible. Let me clarify that the word is not being used in the same manner we often use it today to describe someone who was "inspired" to write a book, paint a painting, or compose a song. We don't mean to say that the Apostle Paul saw a gorgeous sunset, felt moved by its beauty, and then wrote the book of Galatians as a result. First and foremost, when used in this context, inspiration has to do with the fact that the Bible's ultimate author is God. In 2 Timothy 3:16, Paul famously writes, "All Scripture is God-breathed and is useful for teaching, rebuking, correcting and training in righteousness." Let's unpack that a little.

"All Scripture is God-breathed." That powerful phrase is only three words in Greek—*pasa graphē theopneustos*. Sometimes translated as "All Scripture is inspired by God," those words tell us the extent, focus, and source of the Bible's inspiration. *Pasa* indicates that we're talking about "every" or "all." *Graphē* refers to the Old Testament Scripture, which was all of the Bible that was available at the time. Now let's tackle *theopneustos*. This is a compound word made up of *theo*—from *theos*, meaning God—and *pneustos*—from *pneō*, meaning "to breathe" or *pneuma*, meaning "breath." Hence, all (every) Scripture is God-breathed (inspired by God).[35]

This is major. Some say that only certain parts of the Bible are inspired. Maybe Jesus's words are God-breathed, but that's it. Or perhaps anytime the Bible talks about spirituality, that's from God—but not when it talks about history. The problem here, of course, is that this mind-set puts the individual in the position to decide what is from God and what's not. It doesn't work that way, according to the Bible itself, which affirms that *all* Scripture is inspired by God. We can't pick and choose as we like, even though it can be tempting to do so. Every sentence comes from God. The focus of inspiration is the words, the *graphē*. The focus of his inspiration was not the authors but the text. God did not inspire the authors of Scripture to compose deeply spiritual books. Rather, he breathed out the text themselves, the *graphē*. Not just the concepts of the Bible are inspired, but the writings themselves.

Some people question how this could be. To err is human, right? Therefore, what humans write down—including the words of the Bible—is fallible. We're not talking about small mistakes like misspelled words, but rather errors that result in false claims. This objection implies it is necessary to make mistakes to be human. For Christians, there is a good comparison to be made between Jesus Christ (often called the living Word), who is both divine and human, and the Bible, the written Word, which is also both human and divine. Jesus was fully human, and he did not utter anything false. Though the words of the Bible were written by humans, Scripture is still God's true Word. When God gets involved, all bets are off.

But just saying that the Bible is "God-breathed" does not explain how that could have happened. How did God use human authors, with their own personalities, backgrounds, and writing styles to communicate divine

---

At the heart of the Christian faith stands Jesus, and his words and actions serve as the ultimate guiding star for the Christian.

---

truth? We get an insight from the Apostle Peter when he writes, "Above all, you must understand that no prophecy of Scripture came about by the prophet's own interpretation of things. For prophecy never had its origin in the human will, but prophets, though human, spoke from God as they were carried along by the Holy Spirit."[36]

The Greek term translated here as "carried along" is *phero*. In the book of Acts, the same word is used to describe how Paul's ship was caught in a storm and "driven along" by the wind. In an analogous way, the Old Testament prophets were moved by the Holy Spirit and shared God's Word through their own words. Through humans, God spoke. Each person remained a fully conscious human being with thoughts and feelings and experiences of their own. But while they physically recorded the words, the message was not their own. They were recording not their own ideas but the revelations of God, conveying them through their own unique styles.

Contending with Challenging Passages

But if this is true, then what do we do with the uncomfortable and offensive passages like the one I mentioned at the beginning of this chapter—the bears mauling forty-two children? Or why does God instruct the Israelites to eliminate entire people groups? There are plenty of verses like these:

> This is what the Lord Almighty says: 'I will punish the Amalekites for what they did to Israel when they waylaid them as they came up from Egypt. Now go, attack the Amalekites and totally destroy all that belongs to them. Do not spare them; put to death men and women, children and infants, cattle and sheep, camels and donkeys.'[37]

Or how about a verse like this one: "Women should

remain silent in the churches"?[38] The list could go on, but it boils down to this question: If verses like these are in the Bible and the Bible is God's Word, does that mean God is violent and racist and sexist?

As is so often the case, the answer isn't that simple. It's undeniable that the Old Testament is filled with violence and warfare. But it's important to dig more deeply into its role in the history of the Israelites. When we do, we discover that God wasn't randomly "smiting" people left and right. Rather, warfare was used as an instrument of justice. Dr. Norton Herbst explains it this way:

> [God] often used Israel to execute justice upon offenders who had committed acts that even modern people would call evil. This kind of justice values the lives of victims by acting on their behalf, and it values the lives of offenders by taking their actions seriously and dealing with them in the context of their place in human society.
>
> However, though God sometimes used warfare to bring justice upon entire societies and political structures, this does not mean he judged every specific person who was part of that group. The societal values that produced these detestable acts were the target of God's actions. Unfortunately, some innocent people faced the consequences, but such, regrettably, are the ramifications of living in a world entirely corrupted by human evil. . . .
>
> Moreover, the specific context of that unique time period is crucial. In ancient Near Eastern

culture, triumph in warfare was commonly associated with the strength of a nation's god. Consequently, the annihilation of Israel's enemies conveyed that the one true God of Israel had asserted his power and rule over the false gods of other groups.[39]

Again, we are reminded that we must keep in mind that the events outlined in the Bible took place at specific times in human history. We must read texts in their historical context. History tells us that some of these ancient peoples were committing acts of savagery, such as sacrificing children. A more modern analogous example can be found in the use of warfare to stop the Nazi genocide.

It's also both accurate and important to remember that the Bible is often descriptive, not prescriptive. The Bible can describe murder or lying or theft without recommending we model those actions. Not every book, chapter, or verse gives a moral example of how we should live our lives today—though that is not to say that we can't learn from each.

Christians believe that every part of the Bible reveals more about God's character, more about his work in the world, and more about his ultimate plan for the redemption and restoration of the world. This means that we can neither ignore these difficult passages nor lose sight of the larger story Scripture is telling. Throughout the Bible, God extends compassion, grace, mercy, and patience to humankind. Time and again in the Old Testament, we see God show mercy to the people and nations who repented of their wrongdoings.

We see him withhold righteous judgment for several generations, giving people the opportunity to "get it." And in the New Testament, Jesus makes clear that God's message is one of love and forgiveness.

When we encounter verses that offend us or make us uncomfortable, in addition to approaching them with careful scholarship, we do ultimately have to make a choice about how we will take them to heart, what kind of role they will play in our lives, and how they will impact our faith. For the Christian, the best thing to do is refer back to the person of Jesus.

How did Jesus view violence? He commanded that his followers turn the other cheek—resisting violence when possible, while leaving room for righteous indignation at the sight of injustice.[40] How did Jesus treat women? He respected and cared for them as valued, beloved children of God. In fact, immediately following the resurrection, Jesus didn't appear to any of the Twelve Apostles. The first person to see the resurrected Jesus was a woman: Mary Magdalene. And after that? Three more women: Mary the mother of James, Salome, and Joanna were among the first people to see Jesus, and their important role is recorded in the Bible.[41]

At the heart of the Christian faith stands Jesus, and his words and actions serve as the ultimate guiding star for the Christian. When asked which commandment in Scripture was the greatest, Jesus responded confidently and plainly: "'Love the Lord your God with all your heart and with all your soul and with all your mind.' This is the first and greatest commandment. And the second is like it: 'Love your neighbor as yourself.' All the Law and the Prophets hang on these two commandments."[42] That is, the entirety of Scripture hangs on these two commands: Love God. Love others.

The fact is, the Bible is very clear that God came to earth through Jesus for the whole world—regardless of their ethnicity, their gender, or their past. The crux of the matter can be summed up in this sentence from Peter, who received a vision from God about all this. "I now realize," he writes, "how true it is that God does not show favoritism but accepts from every nation the one who fears him and does what is right."[43]

The Transformative Power of Scripture

There will always be elements of mystery surrounding the Bible. There are things we simply don't know until we know them. Things we don't understand until, suddenly, we do. One night, I was in a discussion group with a few people, including my friend Phil, who considered himself an atheist for decades. As part of our conversation, we were reading Romans 10. At one point, Phil abruptly said out loud, "That's it. I got it." A sudden, profound clarity overcame him, as if God was speaking directly to him. We've remained friends and I've watched his mind, heart, and life transform for the better since that evening.

That's just one anecdote. Phil is neither the first nor the last to experience the swift, unexpected arrival of comprehension. Like the first time a new math equation clicks or that moment when you finally make sense of the instruction manual, clarity hits with sweet relief and perhaps even a whoop of joy. It may seem unbelievable or too simple to be true, but this very phenomenon has affected theologians, scholars, educators, students . . . and even yours truly. According to person after person, it feels almost as if the text captured within the pages of the Bible holds a supernatural power. It's as if the verses are speaking directly to you. Hebrews 4:12 says, "The word of God is alive and active. Sharper than any double-edged sword, it penetrates even to dividing soul and spirit, joints and marrow; it judges the thoughts and attitudes of the heart."

Scripture is alive and active. We read in the Bible that Scripture is our food,[44] our life,[45] our comfort,[46] our strength,[47] our guidance,[48] our desire,[49] our hope,[50] our love,[51] our joy,[52] and our treasure.[53] Its words can melt hearts[54] and change lives." Scripture can refresh you,[55] grant you wisdom,[56] fill you with joy,[57] and give you strength to stand against sin.[58] And the fact of the matter is, these aren't just empty promises. There are stories behind each of these qualities. And real people behind each of those stories. The Bible itself is full of stories of unlikely heroes and lives forever changed:

> Within the pages of the Bible, a murderer becomes a leader, a prostitute the ancestor of a spiritual hero, a dishonest tax collector a benefactor, a shy guy an instructor, and a callous religious zealot an ambassador of faith. Barren women become mothers of important children; cowardly fishermen become spokesmen for reformation; people with

pronounced impediments become messengers for God.[59]

The transformative power of God's Word is alive and well today. The Bible encompasses a beautifully paradoxical commingling of variety and unity. Sixty-six books written over thousands of years by dozens of authors from different locations in three different languages, using multiple literary genres to cover a wide range of topics . . . and yet the Bible tells one unified story. A tale not just of ancient people and faraway lands but a grand, sweeping story of God's relationship with humanity. It begins with creation and ends with the promise of a full restoration, a re-creation of this world, with God and his creation living together in full harmony. Front and center stands Jesus, savior and Messiah. Ultimately, the Bible tells the story of God's love for us. That means you and me, directly and specifically. Christians believe the story isn't over—nowhere near it.

Endnotes for Chapter 6

1. Friedrich Paulsen, *Immanuel Kant: His Life and Doctrine*, trans. James Edwin Creighton and Albert Lefevre (New York: Charles Scribner's Sons, 1902), 48.
2. Howard G. Baetzhold and Joseph B. McCullough, eds., *The Bible According to Mark Twain* (Athens, GA: University of Georgia Press, 1995), 227.
3. *The Holy Bible*, New International Version © 2011, 2 Kings 2:24. Refer to 2 Kings 2:23 for more context in this unusual story of the prophet Elisa.
4. The Hebrew Bible contains twenty-four books. They are divided differently in the Protestant Old Testament, making a total of thirty-nine books. Catholics include the Apocrypha, which adds another seven books to their Bible.

5. Norton Herbst, PhD, "What Is the Bible?" Explore God, https://www. exploregod.com/articles/what-is-the-bible. For more comprehensive descriptions of these genres, consult Gordon D. Fee and Douglas Stuart, How to Read the Bible for All Its Worth, 3rd. ed. (Grand Rapids, MI: Zondervan, 2003).

6. J. I. Packer, *God Has Spoken: Revelation and the Bible* (Ada, MI: Baker Academic, 1994), 109.

7. Numbers are accurate as of October 2019. See "Latest Bible translation statistics," Wycliffe Bible Translators, https://www.wycliffe.org.uk/about/our-impact/.

8. Leland Ryken, "The Bible as cultural influence," *Washington Times*, December 11, 2014, https://www.washingtontimes.com/news/2014/dec/11/the-bibles-influence-the-bible-as-cultural-influen/.

9. The Merneptah Stele and other archaeological evidence support the fact that, in the late thirteenth century, Israelites were agriculturalists who were relatively well established in Canaan. Moreover, the very fact that Israel is mentioned in the inscription alongside major city-states indicates that it was a significant force in the region, again corroborating the biblical narrative. For more information, see Michael G. Hasel, "Israel in the Merneptah Stela," *Bulletin of the American Schools of Oriental Research*, no. 296 (Nov 1994): 45–61. However, some scholars argue that "seed" refers not to Israel's grain supply but to Israel's progeny, which would signify that the Israelites were likely pastoralists, as opposed to settled, crop-growing agriculturalists.

10. *The Holy Bible*, 1 Kings 22:39.

11. Ken A. Kitchen, *On the Reliability of the Old Testament* (Grand Rapids, MI: Eerdmans, 2003), 338.

12. See *The Holy Bible*, Genesis 24:10–64.

13. See *The Holy Bible*, Genesis 12:1–3.

14. Nelson Glueck, *Rivers in the Desert: A History of the Negev* (New York: Farrar, Straus and Cudahy, 1959), 136. For much more detail, see Kenneth A. Kitchen, *On the Reliability of the Old Testament* (Grand Rapids, MI: Wm. B. Eerdman's Publishing Co., 2003)..

15. *Acts of Pontius Pilate* has not been found, but it's highly unlikely that Justin Martyr would publicly request the consultation of records if he was not confident they existed.

16. Bart D. Ehrman, *Whose Word Is It?* (London: The Continuum International Publishing Group, 2006), 211.

17. For a detailed account of specific ancient documents and a chart comparing the time gaps and numbers of manuscripts available, see Dr. Josh D. McDowell and Dr. Clay Jones, "The Bibliographical Test," updated August 13, 2014, adapted from Clay Jones, "The Bibliographical Test Updated," *Christian Research Journal*, vol. 35, no. 3 (2012), https://www.josh.org/wp-content/uploads/Bibliographical-Test-Update-08.13.14.pdf.

18. McDowell and Jones.

19. Bruce M. Metzger and Bart D. Ehrman, *The Text of the New Testament: Its Transmission, Corruption, and Restoration* 4th ed., (New York: Oxford, 2005), 51.

20. See *The Holy Bible*, Genesis 1:11-27.

21. *The Holy Bible*, Genesis 2:5.

22. Kenneth A. Mathews, *The New American Commentary Volume 1A Genesis 1–11:26* (Nashville: Broadman & Holman Publishers, 1996), 194.

23. Craig Keener, PhD, "A Deeper Look at If the Bible Is Reliable," Explore God, https://www.exploregod.com/articles/a-deeper-look-at-if-the-bible-is-reliable. "According to the most widely accepted theory, Matthew and Luke both used Mark as a source. Comparison shows that they usually followed Mark closely, sometimes supplementing with information from another shared source. This overlap in material resembles what we find among other ancient biographers. And just as those biographers tried to depend on sources that they believed were trustworthy, Matthew and Luke undoubtedly deemed Mark an accurate source. Because they wrote relatively soon after Mark did, they were in a good position to know how precisely Mark had followed his sources (according to early tradition, his primary source was Peter). . . . By the time that Luke writes, he knows of "many" written accounts about Jesus (Luke 1:1). . . . Two years was certainly ample time for Luke to do what he claimed he did—confirm many of the widely circulated accounts about Jesus (Luke 1:4). That Luke claims to confirm the stories about Jesus makes clear that he is not simply making them up; the bulk of what he had to say was already circulating by his day. That is clear because one does not normally appeal to an audience's fairly extensive knowledge of events if, in fact, one's audience has no such knowledge."

24. John M. Frame, *The Doctrine of the Word of God (A Theology of Lordship)* (Phillipsburg, NJ: P&R Publishing, 2010), 184.

25. Tradition states that the Septuagint was translated by seventy-two scholars (six from each of the twelve tribes of Israel), who each translated the text independently. Ultimately, all the scholars produced identical translations.

26. For a list of specific English translations and their respective approaches to translation, see Norton Herbst, PhD, "Why Are There So Many Bible Translations?" Explore God, https://www.exploregod.com/articles/why-are-there-so-many-bible-translations

27. "FAQ," Wycliffe Bible Translators, https://www.wycliffe.org.uk/about/faq/.

28. Scholars theorize that the scrolls were hidden for protection by the local community as tensions between the Jews and Romans rose. In 70 CE, Titus invaded Israel and destroyed the Temple in Jerusalem. Roman forces occupied the Qumran community, and so the scrolls remained hidden until a shepherd discovered them while searching for his lost animal.

29. Archaeologists examined pottery, coins, graves, and clothing; they arrived at a date range of the second century BCE to the first century CE.

Paleographers and orthographers studied the writing style and spellings and arrived at a range of the third century BCE to first century CE. Radiocarbon demonstrates that the scrolls range from the fourth century BCE to the first century CE.

30. Gleason Archer, *A Survey of Old Testament Introduction*, rev. ed. (Chicago: Moody Press, 2007), 29.

31. See *The Holy Bible*, Isaiah 55:8.

32. "Creeds, Early," in *A Dictionary of Early Christian Beliefs* (Peabody, MA: Hendrickson Publishers, Inc, 1998), 181-183.

33. *The Holy Bible*, John 7:15.

34. *The Holy Bible*, Matthew 4:1-11.

35. For more detailed explanation, see the commentary by Greek scholar George Knight, who concludes, "Paul appears to be saying, therefore, that all scripture has as its source God's breath and that this is its essential characteristic. This is another way of saying that scripture is God's word (cf. Jesus' use of 'scripture' and 'word of God' in apposition to each another in Jn. 10:35." George W. Knight, *The Pastoral Epistles: A Commentary on the Greek Text* (Grand Rapids, MI: W. B. Eerdmans, 2013), 447.

36. *The Holy Bible*, 2 Peter 1:20-21.

37. *The Holy Bible*, 1 Samuel 15:2-3.

38. *The Holy Bible*, 1 Corinthians 14:34.

39. Norton Herbst, PhD, "Why Did God Murder So Many People?" Explore God, https://www.exploregod.com/articles/why-did-god-murder-so-many-people. "For example, the aforementioned Amalekites had attacked the Israelites in an especially atrocious way. Moses reminded the Israelites: 'When you were weary and worn out, [the Amalekites] met you on your journey and attacked all who were lagging behind; they had no fear of God' (Joshua 6:21). Rather than wage war against Israel's army, the Amalekites attacked the women, children, sick, and elderly after the soldiers and healthy men had passed by. Other nations that Israel fought practiced child sacrifice, tortured prisoners of war, and engaged in perverse sexual acts against women (Deuteronomy 25:17-18)."

40. Mark 11:15-27 tells the story of Jesus's righteous indignation upon seeing the temple courts being treated as a market.

41. All four gospels agree that Mary Magdalene was the first to see the risen Christ. Matthew, Mark, and Luke all mention Mary the mother of James. Mark names Salome, while Luke mentions Joanna.

42. *The Holy Bible*, Matthew 22:37-40.

43. *The Holy Bible*, Acts 10:34-25. An in-depth scholarly, historical, and literary analysis of seemingly offensive passages reveals harmony with the words and character of Jesus. For more information, see Walter C. Kaiser, Peter H. Davids, F.R. Bruce, and Manfred Brauch, *The Hard Sayings of the Bible* (Downers Grove, IL: InterVarsity Press, 2010).

44. See *The Holy Bible*, Deuteronomy 8:3; Matthew 4:4; Jeremiah 15:16.

45. *The Holy Bible*, Deuteronomy 32:46-47.

46. See *The Holy Bible*, Psalm 119:50, 52.

47. See *The Holy Bible*, Psalm 119:28.

48. See *The Holy Bible*, Psalm 119:105.

49. See *The Holy Bible*, Psalm 119:20, 40, 131.

50. See *The Holy Bible*, Psalm 119:43, 74, 81, 114, 137; 130:5.

51. See *The Holy Bible.*, Psalm 119:97, 127, 140, 159, 167.

52. See *The Holy Bible*, Jeremiah 15:16; Psalm 1:1-2; Psalm 119:14, 16, 47-48; John 15:11.

53. See *The Holy Bible*, Psalm 119:72.

54. See *The Holy Bible*, Jeremiah 23:29.

55. See *The Holy Bible*, Psalm 19:7.

56. See *The Holy Bible*

57. See *The Holy Bible.*, Psalm 19:8.

58. See *The Holy Bible*, Psalm 19:9-11.

59. Creig Marlowe, PhD, "Is the Bible Still Relevant?" Explore God, https://www.exploregod.com/articles/is-the-bible-still-relevant.

CHAPTER SEVEN

Can I Know God Personally?

"Why is it when we talk to God, we're said to be praying—
but when God talks to us, we're said to be schizophrenic?"
—Jane Wagner, written for Lily Tomlin

This chapter's question presses on me more than any of the others, especially in moments of solitude. I want to know if God is accessible, personal, and relational. If God is out there, can I connect with him? If I talk to him, does he listen? Does he talk back? It seems wild to think we could have a relationship with God, doesn't it? Especially when you consider the idea in light of our human relationships. We can't see God or hug God or shake God's hand. We're humans and God is . . . well, God. What could we possibly offer God? Why would God ever want anything to do with us? Do you ever wrestle with these kinds of questions?

I have some friends who tell me that if they ever walked into a church, the building would probably catch on fire. They think they've done way too much "bad" stuff for God to want them around. Perhaps you're one of the many of us who carry so much guilt and shame—often skillfully covered with humor or nonchalance—that you sincerely think you're too far gone for God to connect with you, if he even wanted to. You're scared that you're irredeemable. *If there is a knowable God,* you may think, *I'm definitely not the kind of person he wants to know.* I've also had people tell me that they're afraid to try to get to know God because of what they might find and how that might impact them. Knowing God might mean changing the way they live their lives. Guilt, shame, and fear are powerful forces, aren't they?

But here's the thing: I have experienced the reality of a personal relationship with God. I have lowered the mask that I sometimes put on for other people, dropped the facade that makes it look like I know what I'm doing, and reveled in the sweet relief of God's grace for a flawed man like me. There are certain things about myself that I don't share with anyone—sometimes not even my wife. There are unkind feelings and ugly thoughts tumbling around in me. There is pride and apathy and envy. Unfortunately, the efforts I put into hiding those aspects of my character construct barriers that prevent true connection. But I have come to realize that the God of the Bible wants to tear down those walls, shed light on all the dark places of my heart, and build a relationship based in love, truth, and grace.

As Christians understand it, God creates each person with great care, love, and concern for the individual. Because God cherishes each of us, he longs for us to seek out a relationship with him. The Bible tells us that God has been communicating with men and women since creation, and it assures us that he remains accessible and knowable. God is still involved in his creation—and we can experience him through a personal relationship.

The Relational God

Just who is this God? And why does he want to have a relationship with us? Christians believe the answers to those questions are rooted in the Trinity, which can be a tricky concept to grasp. The doctrine of the Trinity says that there is only one true God, and that God exists in three distinct persons: the Father, the Son, and the Holy Spirit (or Holy Ghost).

Christians have always maintained their monotheistic belief in one God. But they also claim *Jesus* is God. As we've discussed, Jesus's early followers prayed to him, sang hymns to him, praised him, and worshipped him as God because of his teachings, miracles, and resurrection. Christians continue to do so to this day. And yet, Jesus himself prayed to God as his Father. He talked of God the Father as distinct from the Son. On top of *that,* as the day of his death approached, Jesus told his followers, "I will ask the Father, and he will give you another advocate to help you and be with you forever—the Spirit of truth."[1] And *then,* Jesus left his followers with a mission: "Therefore go and make disciples of all nations, baptizing them in the name of the Father and of the Son and of the Holy Spirit."[2] This is foundational to the Christian understanding of who God is and how we can come to know him.

The Trinity does not mean that God changes forms, some days preferring to be the Father and other days choosing to be the Son. It doesn't mean that God the Father is somehow in charge of two lesser divine beings, the Son and the Holy Spirit. It doesn't mean that there are three Gods. So, what *does* it mean? Ultimately, the Trinity is a divine mystery best grasped through faith. But though material analogies fall far short, they can be helpful in working to grasp this concept.[3] Saint Patrick famously used the clover to illustrate the three-in-one nature of God: one leaf represents the Father, one the Son, and one the Spirit. Three leaves, one clover. Saint Augustine pointed to the human mind, which is made up of memory, understanding, and will but remains a unified whole. Each of these examples attempts to demonstrate how God can be one being existing in three interdependent "persons" who are each equally God.

But there's another way to look at the question of the Trinity, based on a simple Bible verse: "God is love."[4] This means God didn't begin to experience love only after plants, animals, and humans entered the picture. He *is* love. Theologian Jonathan Edwards explained it this way: "The very essence of God's reality is the intratrinitarian love of the Father, Son, and Holy Spirit. . . . The only possible reason for such a being to create the universe was to extend that love to other, imperfect, beings."[5] From this perspective, we see that God created humankind expressly to extend love—that is, to extend himself—to his creation. What he offers to us is relationship built on the overflow of the love that exists innately within him. Time and again within the pages of the Bible, we see God state plainly that his desire is for us to be his people and for him to be our God.[6] God was, is, and always will be in relationship through the persons of the Trinity—relationship exists at the very core of God. This is a God of relationship who created us for loving relationships with each other and with him.

Searching for God

If that's the case, though, why does it often feel so difficult to find God? Since the beginning of time, humans have searched for God. People have done this in a variety of ways, but exploring religion is a natural starting point. Unfortunately, God isn't always what we encounter when we check out religious organizations. All too often, we instead discover people who profess their faith with their lips but fail to live it out with their actions. We are confronted with hypocrisy, indifference, and pettiness. We see faith used as an excuse to treat others as inferior people—or we experience that firsthand. When a religion incorporates the belief that all people are created in God's image to be his representatives (as Christianity does), the actions of its adherents become that much more significant. And it becomes even more disappointing, disruptive, and damaging when those actions demonstrate a disconnect from God's character and the beliefs being espoused.

You don't have to be in a church building to find God.

In these instances, religion is less about God and more about humans. The experience is less about finding, knowing, and honoring God and more about impressing or performing for other people. When we step back, we can see that this kind of religion is largely a human construct that obscures our view of God rather than a transformative force that connects us to God and helps us learn who God is. Though I cherish the invaluable role church has played in my life and the lives of countless others, I also know that you don't have to be in a church building to find God. If you've tried church after church and determined that you simply can't find God there, fear not: Christians believe that God is omnipresent.

This means God exists everywhere at all times, unrestricted by time or space. King David wrote in one of his psalms, "If I go up to the heavens, you are there; if I make my bed in the depths, you are there. If I rise on the wings of the dawn, if I settle on the far side of the sea, even there your hand will guide me."[7] There isn't a particular place you have to go to find God; rather, there's not a single place you can go where you *can't* find God. Believe it or not, God can be found in a bar on Saturday night as well as in a church on Sunday morning. But many people experience a uniquely powerful, immensely moving connection to God when they join with other believers in a worship setting. In Matthew 18:20, Jesus explains why this is: "For where two or three gather in my name, there am I with them." When we come together with others who are also pursuing a relationship with God, God is there in our midst.

The God Who Seeks You

Christians believe that we haven't always had such a hard time finding and connecting with God. Let's recap a bit. In the beginning, humans walked with God. We talked together openly face to face. All was as it was meant to be. But with a devastating act of disobedience, the harmonious coexistence of God and humans was broken. Sin entered the picture, and we began to hide from the one who made us. Creation gave way to destruction, and we were separated from God in the world—both physically and spiritually. Nothing in our power can ever repair the damage done in that moment. Since then, each of us has sinned plenty ourselves. Not one of us consistently lives up to even our own moral standards for ourselves, much less God's. There's not a single thing a person can do to mend the rift created by that ancient act and its legacy of arrogance, disrespect, and pride. And that might well have been the end of it all.

But remember back in chapter 1 when we talked about King Solomon's quest to find purpose? Do you recall his conclusion in the book of Ecclesiastes? Life without God is meaningless. The pursuit of anything else—pleasure, success, wealth—is simply "chasing after the wind."[8] You'll end up exhausted, sweaty, and grumpy, and you won't once have pinned down the breeze . . . or lasting satisfaction. However, when we stop chasing the winds of this world, we discover a beautiful, paradoxical truth: love, grace, truth, joy, and purpose have been pursuing *us* all along. God didn't let the story end in tragedy.

Christians believe that God is still actively seeking relationship with each of us—relationship built on deep, abiding, restorative love. In his classic nineteenth-century poem "The Hound of Heaven," Francis Thompson describes God as a persistent hunting dog, pursuing us with a steady and deliberate pace.[9] When we abandon our chasing after the wind and allow the Hound of Heaven to "catch" us, we discover that *he* is the one whom we are seeking. By allowing ourselves to be found, we can receive the divine love we know to be lost. Though Thompson's imagery may feel extreme or frightening, his message is one of hope—a hope found in the God who loves actively, unconditionally, and eternally. God is not inaccessible to us, hidden away at the top of a mountain or within a particular church building. God did not set the world in motion and then walk away to watch the show from a theater box in the sky. No. God is actively pursuing reconciliation with us. He never gives up the chase.

The God Who Saves

Jesus says plainly that he "came to seek and save the lost."[10] Who are "the lost" to whom he's referring? All of us. God offers all of us salvation from separation, both in the present and for eternity. The uncomfortable reality is, we could never make ourselves worthy of knowing God. We could never reach God on our own because we can't bridge the gap made by sin. But thankfully, God can—and did.

Though we were once separated, we can now be reconciled to God through Jesus. Because of Jesus, we have the opportunity to know God's mercy, love, and grace for ourselves. Through his sacrificial death, Jesus opened the pathway for each of us to form a direct, personal relationship with God. Through his resurrection, Jesus conquered sin and death, tearing down the barriers that prevented us from accessing God.

Salvation from sin and separation isn't something we can earn, and it's certainly not what we deserve. We could never be "good enough" to save ourselves from our messes. The punishment for sin is death. But Jesus took the sins of the world upon himself and died, taking our punishment upon himself as well. He triumphed over sin and death and so, now can we. Make no mistake: we had nothing to do with any of it. We didn't do anything. But as Christians understand it, if we put our trust in Jesus, we are credited with his righteousness and redeemed by his perfect sacrifice. This is what Christians mean when they say things like, "Jesus paid it all." The Bible puts it this way: "God made him who had no sin to be sin for us, so that in him we might become the righteousness of God."[11]

The God Who Loves

Christians believe that when we choose to accept the gift of salvation, we are forgiven our sins and welcomed into relationship with God—a relationship as close as family. As the Gospel of John says, "To all who did receive him, to those who believed in his name, he gave the right to become children of God."[12]

In fact, Jesus told his followers to pray to God by saying, "Our Father in heaven."[13] In so many ways throughout the Bible, we're shown that God parents his people. He nurtures, protects, and supports. Time and again, he guides them to a better future, delivering messages of truth through people, prophets, and finally, his Son. And like most parents, what God wants most from us is for us to accept his love, live in light and truth, and share that love with others.

Like many people, I found that becoming a parent myself radically changed my understanding of God. Suddenly I was confronted with a love so deep and all-consuming that sometimes it hurt. My children had done nothing to earn that love (and never could). For that reason, they could never lose it. The love came from within me. The same is true of God the Father. If that hasn't been your experience with your dad, take comfort in the words of Jennie Allen: "Sometimes earthly fathers expect us to earn their approval. But God doesn't work that way."[14]

I want to acknowledge, though, that there are certainly times when it doesn't feel like God is loving us—not in the least. When you lose a relationship or a job or your health, you might not feel nurtured, protected, or supported. We all know that pain and suffering are facts of this life. But Christians also know that those times are temporary. Do you remember what we said in chapter 3 about God's plan for redemption? In the "new heaven and new earth" promised by God, pain and suffering cease to be.[15] "God's dwelling place [will be] among the people, and he will dwell with him. . . . 'He will wipe every tear from their eyes. There will be no more death' or mourning or crying or pain, for the old order of things [will have] passed away."[16] According to the Bible, we get a glimpse of what is to come for the world in Jesus's resurrection: the reversal of death and the liberation from decay. This is what will ultimately happen throughout creation. As C. S. Lewis put it, heaven "will work backwards and turn even that agony into a glory."[17]

The God We Can Know

But what can we do to learn more about who God is and what he may want for our lives in the here and now? Just as we grow our connection with people with whom we choose to spend our time, we come to know God by spending intentional time in his presence. With intentionality, vulnerability, and commitment, we can strengthen and deepen our relationship with God.

Knowing God through Prayer

No relationship can ever flourish if the two parties don't talk to each other. And essentially, that's all that prayer is: talking with God. Can it feel weird when you start? Absolutely. Might you feel silly sometimes, even if you've been praying for years? Certainly. Is it worth it? Undoubtedly. The Bible is packed with the prayers of men and women, talking with God about all sorts of things. There are prayers of praise and thanksgiving for what God has done. There are prayers of lamentation and confessions of feeling abandoned, fearful, and anxious. There are prayers of contrition, asking God for forgiveness of sin. At the core of all of them is a surprisingly simple concept: deliberate, honest communication with God. But is it really that easy?

Turns out, it is. You may feel like you need to do something special in order to speak to God—light a candle or play some hymns or put on your Sunday best. But the truth is, you don't *need* to do anything but open your mouth and speak (or think silently or write in a journal or sing). You won't be graded on the words you choose. You won't be quizzed on Bible verses. You won't be judged for what's on your heart. The fact is, God knows the matters of your heart already. He knows what you're struggling with, what's got you down, and what you're excited about. He wants you to share that *with* him of your own accord—not from obligation but from a sincere desire for true connection.

You can speak to God exactly like you'd speak to a parent, friend, or spouse. There are no magic words. There need not be any formality to it. But if you find it overwhelming to start talking out of nowhere, consider looking back at prayers in the Bible. The entire book of Psalms is comprised of prayers—prayers of praise, petition, and mourning. Or you can read Jesus's own prayers in the book of John.[18] There's nothing wrong with beginning with the prayers written by those who came before you, as long as the words of the prayer intertwine with the truths of your heart. Otherwise, as C. S. Lewis said, "A team of properly trained parrots would serve as well as men."[19] If we're not sharing the reality—good, bad, and ugly—of what's going on in our minds and hearts, we've stunted the relationship. Intimacy can't flourish without honesty.

But as in any relationship, we can't just talk. We also have to listen. Imagine you were friends with someone who talked with you about everything going on in their life with brutal honesty and inspiring vulnerability. They shared their struggles, bared their soul, and asked you what they should do . . . but then just walked away, never bothering to listen to your response. Would you consider that a healthy relationship? Of course not.

Now, when I say to stop and listen for God to answer your prayers, I don't mean that you'll hear a voice booming from the heavens (though, hey—anything's possible!). I'm talking about something much subtler. Pastor Hugh Halter offers this advice:

> One thing that's been helpful to me, honestly, is to ask him things and to then be quiet and see what enters my heart and my mind. . . . Ask him specific things. Maybe stop after you ask him something and just see if he speaks back to you—if some impression comes into your heart, and then when it does, try to act on it. And then I think if you will

> do those things, you'll actually start to see that God
> is relating with you. He is communicating with you
> and he will show up in your life.[20]

As in our human relationships, there will be times when we feel closer to God than at other times. Most Christians experience seasons when it feels like they're not connecting with God in prayer. Even Mother Teresa wrote that she had not sensed God's presence in her life for over fifty years: "The silence and the emptiness is so great that I look and do not see, listen and do not hear."[21] And yet she did not abandon her faith. She continued to trust in God's promise. It's easier said than done, but we can follow Mother Teresa's example, keeping faith that God is listening (even if we doubt it at times). In this way, we are able to get through those dry times until we enter a season of deeper connection.

But even harder times come when we desperately ask God for something important to us and he doesn't act on our behalf. When we pray for something like the healing of a loved one, and God does not heal, that can really rock us. If our prayers don't change the outcome of a situation, then what's the point of it at all? Does it really matter? The Christian answer is yes—definitely. We know from the Bible that God does care for us and listen to our prayers, but that doesn't mean he gives us everything we ask for. Just as a parent can't always give a child what he wants, God the Father can't always tell his children yes. Whether we like it or not, whether we understand it or not, God's knowledge so far exceeds our own that we could never fully understand why things happen as they do.

Nor are we intended to use prayer just to make requests of God or influence his will. Prayer is meant to influence us, too. The continual prayer of the Christian is not meant to be an empty action, a box to check off in some sort of spiritual growth to-do list.[22] It's a lifestyle—one that transforms hearts, minds, and spirits over time. The more we talk with God, the more his character is revealed to us. As we come to know God more intimately, we grow, becoming increasingly more like Christ. As a result of that growth, we often can increasingly see the way God has been working in our lives, even when it seemed a prayer went unanswered.

Knowing God through Scripture

One of the best ways to get to know people is by learning who they are, what they've done, and what they plan for the future. The same holds true for getting to know God. Thankfully, the Bible offers us the opportunity to do just that. If the Bible tells the story of God's relationship with humankind, there's no better place to turn when trying to develop your own personal relationship with God. When you read the Bible, you find God's words to the original audience, yes, but you're also uncovering God's words to *you*, directly and individually. In captivating ways, the pages of the Bible can reveal particular truths that relate directly to the specific struggles and triumphs in your life.

You may feel that the tale of the Israelites wandering in the desert or a chronology of the creation of the world doesn't apply to your life today, but woven into every word is the transcendental truth and living light with which God wants to fill your heart. "For everything that was written in the past was written to teach us, so that through the endurance taught in the Scriptures and the encouragement they provide we might have hope."[23] The fact of the matter is, the Bible wasn't written just to inform but also to *transform*.

The more time we spend diving into the pages of the Bible, the more we see the true state of our hearts and minds reflected back at us. As Paul Tripp put it, "The Bible, by its very nature, is heart-revealing."[24] From the way we feel as we read—defensive, inspired, uncomfortable, hopeful—to the way we are convicted to change—to release past bitterness, to pursue Jesus more intentionally, to extend grace to others—the truths of the Bible have the potential to change us from the inside out. As Matt Smethurst writes, "Among other things, we ought to approach Scripture humbly,[25] reverently,[26] desperately,[27] joyfully,[28] expectantly,[29] obediently,[30] and frequently[31]."[32] When we ready our hearts and minds this way, our thoughts, our intentions, and the secret desires we harbor are laid bare before us as we read and apply Scripture. When combining prayer and reading Scripture, you may find that you "hear" insights from the Holy Spirit that connect right to what you are going through at the moment.

If you're not sure where to begin, consider one of the gospels. The books of Matthew, Mark, Luke, and John tell of the life, teachings, death, and resurrection of Jesus Christ. You might start with Mark, the shortest and oldest of the gospels. Or you might begin with the book of John, which takes a more reflective, poetic slant than the other books. After you read about Jesus's life, consider moving on to the book of Acts. Acts details the beginnings of the early Church and follows the Apostles as they share the gospel with the world. The gospels and the Acts of the Apostles comprise the foundation of the Christian faith. From there, you could explore the letters of Paul or you could flip back to immerse yourself in the Psalms.

Wherever you choose to begin, it's imperative that you enter your time of Scripture-reading not with an agenda of your own but with the intent to listen. You're not looking to justify your actions or validate your feelings. You're looking to discover God's Word to you, to hear him (maybe not audibly) speak to *you* through his words to *all*. If you can do this, then you may just find that, as you read, you begin "to know truths you didn't know before" about yourself, God, your relationship with God, and even your relationships with others.[33]

Knowing God through Community

An inescapable truth about humans is that we were created to need and exist within community. One of the first things we see God say about us is, "It is not good for man to be alone."[34] Being in relationship with others helps us see ourselves in a truer light and aids us in our journey of self-growth. All kinds of people—not just the ones with whom we get along but also the people we find annoying, difficult, or infuriating—can refine our characters and elicit positive change in our hearts.

Jesus teaches us how to treat others and how to grow our faith.[35] It's no surprise that neither of these can be learned well on our own. Community offers a natural accountability, a safeguard against loneliness, a consistent source of encouragement and inspiration, and a built-in support system. Christian communities are built around the gospel; therefore, the ultimate goal of a Christian community is to bring each member to a deeper understanding of God's love through the person of Jesus Christ. This is why church can be so instrumental in spiritual growth. "The Church," Jon Tyson says, "when it's working properly, gives people a tangible encounter of what it feels like to be loved by Jesus."[36]

I'm curious. What do you picture when you hear the word "church"? A building with a steeple, stained-glass windows, and uncomfortable pews? A sprawling complex with classrooms, worship centers, and a parking garage? A movie theater? A coffee shop? A garden? The fact is, the Church—with a capital C—has little to do with the physical structure and everything to do with the people. So much so that within Christian theology, the Church, the collective group of believers, is known as the body of Christ. Paul explained it to the early churches like this: "For just as each of us has one body with many members, and these members do not all have the same function, so in Christ we, though many, form one body, and each member belongs to all the others."[37] He continued in 1 Corinthians: "If one part suffers, every part suffers with it; if one part is honored, every part rejoices with it."[38] Christians are meant to live in such deep community with one another that they function as a united whole. The Christian community is intended to be made up of a vast array of people with a vast array of abilities, "so that the body of Christ may be built up until we all reach unity in the faith and in the knowledge of the Son of God and become mature, attaining to the whole measure of the fullness of Christ."[39]

The Church is not and was never intended to be a place of shaming, finger-pointing, victim-blaming, gossiping, or judgment.

Here's where things can get a little uncomfortable. In order to become spiritually mature, we have to come face-to-face with our own sin. And, whether we like it or not, that sin is the concern of the entire community. Before we go any further, let me be perfectly clear in what I mean. The Church is *not* and was never intended to be a place of shaming, finger-pointing, victim-blaming, gossiping, or judgment. The words and actions of members of the body of Christ toward one another should flow from a place of truth, grace, and love.

According to the Bible, the Church is intended to be a community of confession, accountability, encouragement, rebuke, and love.[38] "Brothers and sisters," Paul writes, "if someone is caught in a sin, you who live by the Spirit should restore that person gently. But watch yourselves, or you also may be tempted. Carry each other's burdens, and in this way you will fulfill the law of Christ."[40]

Fewer things are harder than confronting a loved one about a sin or hurt; we're understandably reluctant to do so. We fear the response: retribution, rejection, even rage. And yet the Bible insists that we tackle these issues head-on: "If your brother or sister sins, go and point out their fault, just between the two of you."[41] Go and point out their fault, huh? That doesn't sound like it will be received well, does it? But the risks of ignoring this advice are too great.

When allowed to fester unchecked, sin roots its way into all areas of our lives, corrupting, polluting, and poisoning us and those around us. By practicing loving rebuke, promoting gentle confrontation, and encouraging one another to repent (or turn away) from sin, a community can create a culture of acceptance and grace. This allows members to be honest, open, and transparent with their struggles. Only with this kind of culture can James's guidance be followed: "Confess your sins to each other and pray for each other so that you may be healed."[42]

What does it mean to confess? Confession is simply articulating what's wrong. From there, it is the responsibility of the community to offer active support, encouragement, accountability, love, and truth so that the confessor can find healing and restoration with God. And when others see someone struggling with sin and turning in faith toward God, positive spiritual growth is modeled to them. And so the healthy cycle of confession, encouragement, repentance, and healing continues as the community works to create more opportunities to know God, practice Jesus's teachings, and grow spiritually. This is why, despite its faults (and I admit there *are* plenty of faults), the church community remains one of the most solid environments for positive and lasting spiritual change.

But maybe you or your friends don't feel ready to go to church. Maybe you've attended a church before, had a bad experience, and aren't yet willing to try it again. That's OK. There are plenty of ways to establish community. Christians have been growing together in smaller communities as long as they've been following Jesus. In fact, most of the earliest Christian churches were comprised of groups who met in each other's homes to learn more about Jesus. In the seventeenth and eighteenth centuries, churches began to organize small groups specifically to help individuals grow in their walk with Jesus. The value of small groups has long been recognized. Today, many churches offer small groups with no church attendance requirements.[43]

Does even a small group seem too intimidating right now? No problem! Look at the people around you. Note their attitudes and behaviors. Who do you see who continuously pursues spiritual growth through their personal relationship with God? Who do you know who regularly models Christ-like behavior? What characteristics or habits do they demonstrate that you'd like to develop within yourself? Ask them to help you get there. Spiritual mentors can be an invaluable resource as we work to grow our relationship with God. Find one person with whom you can read the Bible, pray, share your struggles, or even discuss this book. Remember, Jesus said, "For where two or three gather in my name, there am I with them."[44]

Loving God in Return

God makes it clear that this relationship is meant to be a two-way street. He has given, is giving, and will continue to give all of his love to you—and he wants the same from you. Jesus said plainly that we need to invest in our relationship with God with all that we have: "Love the Lord your God with all your heart and with all your soul and with all your mind and with all your strength."[45] Frankly, it's no different than the way we ourselves want to be loved.

Loving God with all of your heart means sharing your heart with him. Divulge your secret dreams, your quiet hopes, your loud rejoicing. Tell him of your gratitude and joy. But also confess when you're overwhelmed, disappointed, and hopeless. Admit when you're jealous and when you're angry—even if God is the one who made you mad in the first place. Apologize when you've made a mistake and keep your heart open to his truths and forgiveness.

Loving God with all your soul means dedicating your life to him. Turn to him when you're questioning what to do and how to spend your money, your time, and your talents. Invite him to shed light on your life and to show you how to live in a way that brings glory to God. Harbor those truths deep within the marrow of your being and strive to live out his commands in faith.

Devote yourself to receiving and sharing God's love.

Loving God with all your mind means filling your mind from a deep wellspring of knowledge about who God is and what he wants for your life. Dive into the search for understanding. Welcome curiosity and be willing to go deeper. Don't be afraid to ask questions, to challenge and wrestle with his commands and your beliefs. True growth comes with growing pains. Seek the answers. Study his words—don't merely read them but truly *study* what is being said. Take a class. Ask for guidance. At all times, work to fix your thoughts on what is true, honorable, right, pure, lovely, and admirable.[46]

Loving God with all your strength means fighting for your relationship every day. Persevere in your efforts to prioritize time spent with God. Stand steadfast in the midst of challenges, in the midst of pain, in the midst of confusion. Be willing to stretch, change, and grow. Hold yourself accountable. Stay honest with yourself, with God, and with your community. Get up when you fall—every time.[47]

The God Who Will Be Found

But of course, none of this means that you'll never again have doubts or struggles or questions. As in any relationship, there are elements of mystery, faith, and risk. I have known God for most of my life and I have a sure confidence in his existence, his presence in my life, and his love for me. But still I have questions. Still I wonder why things are the way they are. Still I struggle to understand. And yet . . . because I know God to be a good, loving God, I am able to trust him.

Recently I spent an extended amount of time alone in the mountains, grappling with God and some of those very things I don't understand. While I was there, God spoke to me in an extremely personal way, assuring me of his unconditional, unfailing love for me. Regardless of my achievements and failings, apart from whether I've been "good enough" (which I could never be) or a "bad person," his love for me remains steadfast. I'm not a crier, but it was such an emotionally vivid experience that I couldn't stop the tears from falling. Tears of joy, gratitude, and humility sprung up from deep within me because my heart was filled with a love far beyond my full understanding.

That breathtaking, life-saving love isn't available just to me. It's not some special deal that comes with being a pastor. God promises everyone, "You will seek me and find me when you seek me with all your heart. I will be found by you."[48] The standing invitation to enter into a personal relationship with God is open to all of us. I encourage you to explore it for yourself.

Endnotes for Chapter 7

1. *The Holy Bible*, New International Version © 2011, John 14:16-17.
2. *The Holy Bible*, Matthew 28:19.
3. For a more in-depth theological look at the Trinity, see Millard J. Erickson, *Making Sense of the Trinity: Three Crucial Questions* (Grand Rapids, MI: Baker Academic, 2000).
4. *The Holy Bible*, 1 John 4:16.
5. George Marsden, *Jonathan Edwards: A Life* (New Haven: Yale University Press, 2003), 191, 443. "Intratrinitarian" is a term used to refer to the relationships between the persons of the Trinity.

6. See *The Holy Bible*, Exodus 6:7; Leviticus 26:12; Jeremiah 7:23, 11:4, 30:22; Ezekiel 36:28.

7. *The Holy Bible*, Psalm 139:8-10.

8. *The Holy Bible*, Ecclesiastes 2:11.

9. Take a look at these lines: "I fled Him, down the nights and down the days; / I fled Him, down the arches of the years; / I fled Him, down the labyrinthine ways / Of my own mind; and in the mist of tears / I hid . . . From those strong Feet that followed, followed after. / But with unhurrying chase, / And unperturbèd pace, deliberate speed, majestic instancy, / They beat. . . . Now of that long pursuit / Comes on at hand the bruit; / That Voice is round me like a bursting sea: . . . 'Whom wilt thou find to love ignoble thee, / Save Me, save only Me? . . . Rise, clasp My hand, and come! . . . I am He Whom thou seekest!'" Francis Thompson, "The Hound of Heaven," in D. H. S. Nicholson and A. H. E. Lee, eds., *The Oxford Book of English Mystical Verse* (Oxford: The Clarendon Press, 1917). Published in November 2000 by Bartleby.com.

10. *The Holy Bible*, Luke 19:10.

11. *The Holy Bible*, 2 Corinthians 5:21.

12. *The Holy Bible,*, John 1:12.

13. *The Holy Bible,*, Matthew 6:9.

14. Jennie Allen, *Nothing to Prove: Why We Can Stop Trying So Hard* (Colorado Springs, CO: WaterBrook, 2017), 33.

15. *The Holy Bible*, Revelation 21:1.

16. *The Holy Bible*, Revelation 21:3-4.

17. C. S. Lewis, *The Great Divorce* (London: Macmillan, 1946), 64.

18. See *The Holy Bible*, John 17.

19. C. S. Lewis, *The World's Last Night and Other Essays* (San Diego, CA: Harvest/HBJ, 1960), 6.

20. Hugh Halter in "God and Prayer," Explore God, https://www.exploregod.com/videos/god-and-prayer.

21. David Van Biema, "Mother Teresa's Crisis of Faith," Time, August 23, 2007.

22. See *The Holy Bible*, 1 Thessalonians 5:16-18.

23. *The Holy Bible*, Romans 15:4.

24. Timothy Lane and Paul Tripp, *Helping Others Change* (Greensboro, NC: New Growth Press, 2005), 2.7.

25. *The Holy Bible*, Isaiah 66:2.

26. *The Holy Bible*, Psalm 138:2.

27. Our spiritual life is both started (James 1:18 and 1 Peter 1:23) and sustained (Matthew 4:4) by God's words. They are a matter of life and death (Deuteronomy 32:46-47). Psalm 119 displays human longing for God's revelation (see especially verses 10, 20, 31, 40, 81, 123, 131, and 174).

28. *The Holy Bible*, Psalm 1:1-2; Jeremiah 15:16; John 15:11.

29. When Christians approach the Bible properly (not "perfectly"), they can expect comfort and strength (Psalm 119:28, 50, 52, 76, 107); encouragement

and hope (Romans 15:4); guidance (Psalm 119:105); assurance (1 John 5:13), and transformation (John 17:17).

30. *The Holy Bible*, James 1:22; 1 John 2:4-5; Psalm 119:4-5, 10, 34, 56, 59-60, 100, 133, 136, 146, 158, 166-68.

31. *The Holy Bible*, Psalm 119:97, 147-48; Colossians 3:16.

32. Matt Smethurst, "How to Study the Bible," Explore God,https://www. exploregod.com/articles/how-to-study-the-bible.

33. Angie Smith in "Can I Know God Personally?" Explore God, https://www. exploregod.com/videos/can-i-know-god-personally.

34. *The Holy Bible*, Genesis 2:18.

35. Chris Morton, "Five Reasons a Small Group Will Help You Grow," Explore God, https://www.exploregod.com/articles/five-reasons-a-small-group-will-help-you-grow.

36. Jon Tyson in "God and Community," Explore God, https://www. exploregod.com/videos/god-and-community.

37. *The Holy Bible*, Romans 12:4-5.

38. *The Holy Bible*, 1 Corinthians 12:26.

39. *The Holy Bible*, Ephesians 4:12-13.

40. *The Holy Bible*, Galatians 6:1-2.

41. *The Holy Bible*, Matthew 18:15. Paul instructs us in how to escalate the issue from there if it continues.

42. *The Holy Bible*, James 5:16.

43. You can also find or start your own Explore God Discussion Group at https://www.exploregod.com/discussion-group.

44. *The Holy Bible*, Matthew 18:20.

45. *The Holy Bible*, Matthew 22:37.

46. See *The Holy Bible*, Philippians 4:8.

47. The structure of this section is based on Ella Hearrean's article "How to Love God," Explore God, https://www.exploregod.com/articles/how-to-love-god.

48. *The Holy Bible*, Jeremiah 29:13-14.

Never Stop Exploring

"Twenty years from now, you will be more disappointed
by the things that you didn't do than by the ones you did do.
So throw off the bowlines. Sail away from the safe harbor.
Catch the trade winds in your sails.
Explore. Dream. Discover."
—H. Jackson Brown Jr.'s mother[1]

You've likely noticed by this point that I enjoy hiking in the mountains. As you know now, many of my biggest moments with God have happened in the mountains, so they hold a special place in my life. But my wife frequently teases me when we're hiking together—and for good reason. I often want to see what's over the next hill. "Let's go just a little further and see what there is to see," I say. Only there is always *another* hill ahead. And on the crest of each hill is *another* beautiful vista that I want to see. Without Tamara reminding me that we eventually have to hike all the way back to where we started, I might keep climbing hill after hill after hill in a vain attempt to satisfy my curiosity. Even though I know I could never climb far enough or long enough to fully "see what there is to see."

I find the same applies to my faith journey. You and I have gone through quite an expedition together in the pages of this book. And yet, still I have more questions— so many more. I bet you do, too. I'm still curious about aspects of God, Jesus, and Christianity. I still wonder why bad things happen to good people. I still question why my life looks the way it does sometimes. I still have moments of doubt and uncertainty. But I'm quite comfortable in my inability to find the answers to all my questions. It doesn't discourage me to think that all knowledge is out of my reach. In fact, it engages my curiosity all the more—just as my love for being in the mountains isn't lessened by the fact that I'll never climb to every peak.

Not having all the answers does not undermine or delegitimize faith.

I am compelled to keep exploring. Investigating one question opens up another three questions that need to be asked. Insights gained illuminate still more questions and thus drive the continued search for more answers. Not having all the answers does not undermine or delegitimize faith. In fact, I firmly believe God wants us to keep seeking, keep asking, keep pursuing both him and his love, which surpasses human knowledge. Author Hannah Brencher reflects on this in her book *Come Matter Here:*

> I think God is big enough for our big questions and our bigger frustrations. The answers may not come dramatically. They may not be right in front of my face. But maybe if I keep going, keep asking all the questions that are laid on my heart, something miraculous might happen. I might find a few answers, or I might find peace in the not knowing. My favorite element of God is the not knowing. I love that about my relationship with God. I love that there are gray areas. I love that I cannot possibly be wise enough to understand all that this life has given me. There are dozens of things reported in the news or taking place in my personal life that leave me raising my hands, shrugging my shoulders, and saying, "I'm not really sure. I don't get it." It's not always mine to get.[2]

I find that even after thirty-six years of marriage, my wife is still a mystery. While I know her much better than I did on that Saturday when we said "I do," there is always more to learn. People are deep, complex, multifaceted creatures. Indeed, I'm still discovering more about *myself*. A new situation, a few conversations with an old friend, a new book or movie, and—bam!—I arrive at fresh realizations about who I am and why I respond to things the way I do. I recently met with a counselor who helped me see how I move into "distress" in stressful situations and why I have conflicts with a work associate who is made differently than I am. It's astonishing how much more we can discover about a person after decades together—even when that person is ourselves.

Now magnify that by infinity. That's how much there is discover about God as we learn who he is. In the face of divine mystery, we can throw up our hands in exasperation or we can choose to continue our faith journey. Our doubts propel us to ask more questions, which leads us to dive into the exploration more deeply, which requires us to wrestle with answers more fully. We read; we talk with others; we think; we pray; we reflect; and, so, we grow.

Though you've come to the end of this book, your exploration of God and challenging spiritual questions won't stop here. Nor should it. In the last chapter, we discussed some of the ways you can continue to explore God. You can read the Bible. Check out a different translation or a study Bible that provides further historical and linguistic context. You can practice prayer. Try out a new way of praying, like reading biblical prayers aloud or praying out in nature. You can pursue community with others who are exploring God. Look for a small group at a local church or start an Explore God Discussion Group of your own. ExploreGod.com has a robust library of resources to help you move forward in your faith journey as you work to discover answers to your hard questions. What questions are challenging you most right now? Start there.

Most importantly, never stop exploring.

Endnotes for Conclusion

1   H. Jackson Brown Jr., comp., *P.S. I Love You: When Mom Wrote, She Always Saved the Best for Last* (Nashville: Thomas Nelson, 1991), 13. Quote is from the author's mother.

2   Hannah Brencher, *Come Matter Here: Your Invitation to Be Here in a Getting There World* (Grand Rapids, MI: Zondervan, 2018), 191.

Acknowledgments

If you enjoyed this book, you owe gratitude to Auburn Layman, who edited every sentence. Her eye for detail, pursuit of sources, and ear for a good-sounding phrase improved the writing significantly.

I'm grateful to Global Media Outreach (GMO) for partnering with me to publish *The 7 Big Questions*. Their heart for giving spiritual insights to people all over the world inspires me.

My wife, Tamara, continually encourages me to write at my best. I thank God for her.

Finally, I acknowledge you, the reader. Communication takes at least two. Thank you for picking up this book. I invite you to keep the conversation going with me or with Global Media Outreach. You can email me at bmiller@cfhome.org. You can contact GMO at info@gmomail.org.

About the Author

Bruce graduated Phi Beta Kappa from the University of Texas at Austin with a BA in Plan II, the Honors Liberal Arts Program; received a master's degree in theology from Dallas Theological Seminary; and did doctoral work at the University of Texas at Dallas in the History of Ideas (focused on philosophical hermeneutics, Hans-Georg Gadamer, an postmodernism). He taught theology for four years at Dallas Seminary.

Alongside a strong team, Bruce started Christ Fellowship (CFhome.com) in McKinney, Texas, where he enjoys serving as senior pastor. Bruce serves his local community in several leadership roles, uniting others to make a difference for the under-resourced.

Bruce and his wife, Tamara, enjoy spending time with their grown children and spoiling their wonderful grandchildren. In his spare time, Bruce loves playing racquetball, using a chainsaw, and sitting by an open fire. He looks forward to hiking in the Rocky Mountains whenever he can get there.

Bruce's heart to see people live more joyful, fulfilled lives sparked the writing of *Your Life in Rhythm*. His love for writing has resulted in several more books, including *When God Makes No Sense* and *Big God in a Chaotic World*. You can learn more about Bruce and his other books at BruceBMiller.com

About Global Media Outreach

Global Media Outreach is a family of online ministries that leverage the power of technology to give every person on Earth multiple opportunities to know Jesus.

In 1995, Walt Wilson sat in a meeting at MIT to discuss the impact of the newly launched World Wide Web. Long before the Internet was available in the palms of our hands, God gave Walt a vision for how this new technology could be used to share the truth and hope of the Gospel with the entire world. In 2004, this became Global Media Outreach (GMO).

GMO has launched several digital ministries, discipleship websites, and advertising campaigns in multiple languages across the world—all allowing the Gospel message to reach the farthest corners of the world. With the introduction of their personal response and discipleship platform, GMO ensured that anyone who connects with a ministry or ad can engage in ongoing one-on-one guidance.

Since its founding, GMO has shared the Gospel billions of times and seen hundreds of millions of people find a personal relationship with Jesus. To learn more about GMO, visit **www.GlobalMediaOutreach.com**.

About Explore God

Explore God is a digital ministry within the GMO family that was created as a safe place for anyone to ask their spiritual questions and find easy-to-understand information. Explore God helps people explore, experience, and engage with God's plans for their life. To accomplish this, the ministry takes on tough faith-based topics and helps people discover answers through credible compelling content.

The Explore God website and social media communities are comprised of original content created by thoughtful experts and explorers from around the world. The 7 Big Questions series on which this book is built is a foundational piece of Explore God. It is available as a video-based discussion group series, as well as in sermon series format.

You can learn more at **www.ExploreGod.com**.

CPSIA information can be obtained
at www.ICGtesting.com
Printed in the USA
LVHW081341211022
731220LV00009B/457

9 781683 160205